William Green

A PICTORIAL BIOGRAPHY

William Green

A PICTORIAL BIOGRAPHY

BY Max D. Danish

Published by INTER-ALLIED PUBLICATIONS

NEW YORK, N. Y.

Produced under the direction of NICHOLAS G. BALINT

Printed in the United States of America
by American Book–Stratford Press, Inc., New York, N. Y.

55

Contents

Acknowledgments

I wish to express profound thanks to Philip Pearl, editor of the "AFL News-Reporter," for his unstinted readiness to meet my constant quest for factual information with a keen and patient understanding of the frame and content of this biography of the president of the American Federation of Labor.

My appreciation is also due to Bernard Tassler, editor of the "American Federationist," who generously placed at my disposal his rich photographic files in order to make the pictorial section of this book as complete as possible.

MAX D. DANISH

Author's Note

THIS "SHORT STORY" of William Green lays no pretense to being a complete biography of the President of the American Federation of Labor. More accurately it is a chronicle of the major events which transpired in American labor during the past four decades, and William Green's role in and reactions to these events, told mostly in his own words, and quoted from his numerous speeches, public statements, and editorial notes in the "American Federationist," which he has edited for nearly 28 years.

A full biography of the long and rewarding career of President Green is yet to be written. His life story—from breaker boy to a topmost position not only in labor but in the greater American community—is not trimmed with "from-rags-to-riches" embroidery. His ideals, beliefs and working methods reflect the solid virtues and the driving force of ground-roots America. It is the story of an American worker who mined coal in a small midwestern town for 23 years and came up to the heights because in him abundant natural gifts blended in perfect union with lofty ethics, an inbred humanity and selfless devotion to the millions who for a full generation have come to identify him as their champion and tireless advocate.

William Green's life has coincided with some of the stormi-est social squalls which rocked the first half of this century. He has taken these tempests with the firm reliance of a pilot who knew his course and would not deviate from it. To have had the opportunity of recapitulating these chapters in the life of William Green in this brief biographical sketch has been both a gratifying inquiry and a distinct pleasure.

WILLIAM GREEN

By Max D. Danish

THE American mould of trade unionism was not built according to theoretical blueprints. It grew from a deeply-imbedded revolt of free men against the raw inequities of a booming industrialism. American labor rejected "pie-in-the-sky" visions and counsels of despair alike. It relied on its inherent power, its economic strength. The grit and obstinacy which characterized this rising trade unionism under the direction of Samuel Gompers and his associates stemmed from an aroused confidence that the grave economic injustices meted out to their fellow workingmen in this land of inexhaustible resources could be righted by collective effort through labor organization.

As self-employed craftsmen gave way to wage-earners and new mushrooming industries split skills into fragments to make room for semi-skilled operatives, membership in the trade union movement grew. Fundamentally, nonetheless, its outlook and policies continued to reflect a single-minded pragmatism—rugged and unyielding—to match the unbending antagonism to union organization which the major employer groups of the land had nakedly and brutally displayed since unionism first made its appearance on the American industrial horizon.

Out of the Mines

The mines of America—like the mines in industrial lands everywhere—have given to our labor movement a generous quota of dynamic leadership. And among this group of leaders who emerged from the mines, William Green, who for the past 28 years has stood at the helm of the American Federation of Labor, years of soul-trying crises and cruel war and postwar periods, rises to a stature all his own.

11

Faced, simultaneously at times, by the grim spectre of internal cleavage, on one hand, and the onslaught of the Red conspiracy, on the other, this coal digger from a small Ohio mining community managed, without melodrama or quasi-dictatorial methods, to steer the great organization entrusted to him sanely and safely.

Above all else, even a casual examination of the career of William Green helps to reveal the refreshingly dominant fact that he has never envisaged the top spot in America's labor movement, which he occupies, as a mandate for personal power but as a task service to the millions of his fellow trade unionists and to his country—a task to which he has been happy to give his all.

A "Speech of Acceptance"

When on December 19, 1924, William Green, then secretary-treasurer of the United Mine Workers and a third vice-president of the American Federation of Labor, was notified by the Federation's Executive Council that he had been chosen AFL president for the ensuing yearly term, following the unexpected death of Samuel Gompers on December 13 of that year, he said: "The call which has come to me came as an unsought call for service . . . We shall seek to organize the unorganized . . . Our movement has created great traditions, it has become to all Americans a great bulwark of human freedom . . . There has been left to all of us a legacy of inestimable value which will serve to chart our course."

William Green's brief "speech of acceptance" was as shorn of pomp as the man who uttered it. His simple pledge to organize the men and women still outside the fold of the Federation was a prescribed duty. The legacy he was referring to, obviously, was the philosophy and the trade union "way of life" which Samuel Gompers indelibly stamped upon the American Federation of Labor.

"We Who Know Him Best"

A few weeks prior, at the El Paso convention of the AFL, John L. Lewis, William Green's chief in the Miners' Union, in a speech nominating Green for the third vice-presidency of the Federation, had declared: "I need not at this convention extoll the virtues or accomplishments of William Green, the secretary-treasurer of our great international organization, because many of you have learned to know him through years of attendance at these conventions and have for him that deep affection as a trade unionist in which he is held by his colleagues in his own organization.

"Suffice it to say that we who work with him—and we perhaps know him best—have come to have a profound admiration for his capabilities as an officer, for his fealty to the ideals of the trade union movement, for his stalwart characteristics as a citizen of our country, and for the great good he has been able to perform in the trade union movement and in the civic councils of our nation."

To the thousands, leaders and rank-and-filers alike, who have come to know William Green in the long years of his presidency of the AFL both as the Federation's top executive and as the custodian of the union's prestige, the portrait of William Green as presented to the world by John L. Lewis in the fall of 1924 remains sharply etched, indelible and inviolate.

Early Years

William Green's father, Hugh, an English coal miner, had brought his slender Welsh bride, Jane, to Coshocton, a small mining and farming town in Central Ohio, in 1870, hoping for a better life in the New World. Like countless thousands of others who came to America from the world's older continents with high hopes of opportunity and plenty for all, the Hugh Greens found in Coshocton only the primitive environs of a new continent and the hardships of building a new community.

The local miners' union, a branch of the Progressive Miners Union which later became part of the United Mine Workers, was the only focal point in their life which linked the Greens spiritually with the Old World and brought some sense of security to them, in addition to religion, another spiritual mainstay of the family. The Greens were deeply religious, and Baptist Hugh Green gathered his family together every evening for an hour of prayer.

Their first son, William, was born in a miner's shack, but by the time he could walk the family moved to a house on what was known as Hardscrabble Hill and had settled, with thanks to the Lord, into the life of toil and enforced frugality which was the lot of the American miner in the 1870's. Hugh Green, a slim, silent man, with long white hair and beard, made a dollar and a half a day. By the standards of the town and the times he cared for his family well. There was always enough to eat, there were few luxuries, and life in the town was simple—Bill collected acorns for marbles. Nothing ever happened to cause excitement, except that gruesome standby of a coal town, the mine accident.

A Miner at 16

Bill Green began earning money for his own petty needs from the time he was ten. When he was fourteen, the railroad headed for Central Ohio reached Coshocton and Bill got a job as a water boy for a railroad gang. At sixteen, one early morning he walked the two-and-a-half miles to Morgan Run Mine No. 3, where his father worked, and went down the shaft with him. He learned fast and soon became a full-fledged miner and a good one—for many years he was one of two coal diggers who drew the biggest pay at Morgan Run.

"I started mining coal," William Green later wrote,* "at sixteen as the normal course of life and without any feeling of self-pity on my part. On the contrary, I was glad to take on a man's work that I might have some income to add to the family's purse. That was before the days of the safety lamp or electricity. I helped father to get out the coal he loosened and loaded it into cars to be carried up. I watched him work, and then he let me begin to use the tools. When I was able to use them I bought my own—at the company store. It was all hand work then. Working with my father I learned my trade."

Bill Green knew only what a one-room school in Coshocton had

* "Labor and Democracy," by William Green, 1939.

taught him, but he early developed a hunger for books and he also acquired a flair for oratory in church social debates. His father advised him to study for the ministry, and Bill readily agreed. But though he saved his pay he could not raise the money for the schooling. When he was 22, he married Jennie Mobley, a neighboring miner's daughter, and resigned himself to going on in the mine.

Envelopes—With Puny Pay

Bill Green started going to union meetings with his father as soon as he went into the mines, and, as a matter of course, became a member. His lessons in practical unionism started early for young, sedate Bill Green as he plunged at once into unraveling some of the causes of discontent around the mine. On pay-days the miners got envelopes which contained but little money. The company owed them for the coal they had mined, which was recorded in tons. The company, however, weighed only such coal as remained after it passed over the mine-screen. Sometimes there seemed to be less credit given them than what they knew they had got out, but, of course, the miners could not prove their claim. They would owe the company for house rent, for food and clothing bought at the company store, perhaps a payment for the company doctor, for powder and for sharpening tools. And since their pay never reached above $1.50 a day, there was little real money coming to them.

There were many other disputes over weighing coal, until the union elected a pit committee and it was arranged to have a union man act as a check-weighman to check the records of the mine weighman. There was the other basic problem as to what should be weighed. Miners received no pay for the coal that went through the screen, although it could be sold on the open market. Feeling cheated, they contended that they should be paid on a run-of-the-mine basis the tonnage before deductions were made. This barefaced short-changing of the miners remained an unmitigated evil for years, until as a member of the Ohio State Senate in 1911, William Green introduced a bill abolishing the mine-screen. The battle was fierce but the bill was passed

15

and became law. Similar bills were later passed by the legislatures of other mining states.

"From Cradle to Grave"

In those early days, mine workers paid a considerable share of the expenses of mining. The power of the company surrounded the miner on all sides, literally from cradle to grave. Bill Green kept going regularly to his union's meetings—one of the few opportunities he had for meeting people—soaking up eagerly in his young and receptive mind the woes and problems of his neighbors and his own folks. He learned to speak up, ventured to ask questions or to offer suggestions, and soon became a member of the local's several committees. Then, in quick succession, the local began electing him to office—secretary, treasurer and president.

By modern standards, Morgan Run No. 3 was a terrible place—timbering was bad, cave-ins were frequent and gas hung in its tunnels. The whole mining village of Coshocton lived in fear of mine accidents. Life could be snuffed out in the darkness of the mine at any time. In the 1890's miners could get no insurance to tide their families over the loss of the breadwinner. Bill Green helped to carry out of the mine the crushed bodies of more than one miner. The only source of help to which miners could turn with any sense of friendly response was the union; but the local union was still too weak to stand up to the company.

Oftentimes, the only escape for men goaded and battered on all sides seemed the strike, as the quickest way to revenge. "Men on strike are capable of unrestrained violence," Green wrote years after. "I have known them to call out the maintenance men and leave the mines to flood. In Ohio there are mines which were set on fire during the strike of 1884 still burning more than 50 years later. My temper was no milder than those of my fellow workers, but I saw that it had to be controlled. As a union officer, the significance of collective bargaining grew stronger and ever stronger in my mind. How much further, indeed, we could get by using our heads than by using our fists." The idea of collective agreements, as the only way out of the morass of despair and ineffectiveness inherent in single-mine dealings with mine owners and their managers, thus settled early in the mind of young Bill Green.

At the Head of Ohio Miners

By 1900, William Green, after having made the grade as president of his own Coshocton local and later of the sub-district of the area, became president of District 6, embracing all of Ohio. A persistent and effective negotiator, counseling the middle of the road and invariably blunting the extremists, his influence grew. As District 6 went on strike and Green saw his Ohio miners defeated by trainloads of coal coming in from West Virginia and Pennsylvania, he realized that unless some way of coordinating collective bargaining in the various districts was found, the union miners in the various regions would be merely competing against each other in favor of the coal operators.

He found the answer to this problem in what is still known as the Central Competitive Agreement, a pact covering the UMW districts in Ohio, West Pennsylvania, Indiana and Illinois and negotiated with the joint coal operators of that territory. This agreement, in turn, became the basis of negotiation in all other fields. It worked to stabilize the industry and to raise standards of living for the miners. And although over the years, individual coal operators, aided by recurring business depressions, had tried to upset these centralized pacts in order to gain some immediate special advantages, the principle of the Central Competitive Agreement and its collective machinery survived.

A Training School for Democracy

Young William Green, who in time grew to be a master parliamentarian, had found the union a good training school for acquiring the techniques of cooperating with other human beings in a democratic way. Without rules of order, mine union meetings of that day were likely to be turned quickly into mobs of strong men who paid little attention to union business. With Bill Green wielding the gavel, miner

17

meetings, on any level—local, sub-district or district—had to be orderly and businesslike. "Parliamentary law is, of course, only a means to an end, but it is a necessary tool for group activity," he insisted.

As president of District 6 he met frequently with employers and public officials to adjust grievances and work out problems. There, too, he began to learn the operators' side of industry in addition to the miners' side which he knew well. District president William Green was learning that good times for the miners were bound up with prosperity for mine operators. Interdependence of welfare, he became convinced, was inescapably bound up with techniques of cooperation in working out joint problems and straightening out joint kinks.

Statistician, Senator

In 1910, William Green, by that time already widely known through Central Ohio as the hard-working and wideawake president of District 6, took time out to run for the presidency of the UMW. Things had not been going well in international headquarters, the union's relations with the employers were too tense for comfort, and the Central Competitive Agreement was in danger. He received the support of the younger element in the organization and waged a vigorous campaign, but was defeated. Commented William Green on the outcome: "The kind of work miners do breeds daring but also a fundamental honesty that will not permanently tolerate injustice. I made the fight for those who wanted honesty in our International."

In 1911, John P. White of Iowa became president of UMW, and he appointed William Green international statistician. This position involved gathering of data to be used in collective bargaining, data on mining accidents, accident prevention and information on occupational diseases. He was also appointed a member of the miners' committee to cooperate with the Mine Bureau which was charged by the federal government with promoting safety in the mines. That same year, yielding to demands by large groups of citizens in Coshocton and adjacent counties, William Green became the candidate of the local Democratic Party for the State Senate of Ohio and was elected. In the

18

Ohio Senate, he was chosen floor leader of the party and when the presiding officer of the Senate, Lieutenant Governor Pomerene, resigned to accept a designation to the United States Senate, Green succeeded him as president. While in the Senate, Green continued to serve as the union's statistician and was reelected for another term. On August 1, 1913, however, he became secretary-treasurer of the United Mine Workers, a position which required an enormous amount of concentration and plain hard work. He held that post until 1924 when he became president of the AFL.

Battles in West Virginia

During the 11 years as "finance minister" of the miners' union, following his two years in the Ohio Senate, William Green absorbed a world of new experiences. It was a period when the mine workers were waging a desperate struggle for the right to organize, especially in the hills and valleys of West Virginia. At the first signs of revolt, the coal operators would evict the miners and import carloads of gun-toting Baldwin-Felts hoodlums to intimidate the strikers. During these recurrent strikes, William Green would become the union's chief commissary, would lease lands, organize tent colonies, and provide food for the men and their families.

He likes to tell about one such case in the course of which the coal operators turned to the federal courts for an injunction to break a West Virginia strike. They asked Judge Anderson, a notorious union hater of that period, to order the UMW not to feed the strikers, and the judge announced that he would issue the injunction. As UMW secretary-treasurer, Green, who was directly charged with the task of feeding the strikers, rose in the courtroom and told the judge that "His Honor," obviously, did not fully grasp the implications of the order he intended to issue. "Your Honor, these families are the wards of our international union. Every scrap of food they have we buy for them. We cannot let these women and children die. If you issue the injunction, I must choose whether to obey it and let the miners and their families starve or violate it and go to jail. Your Honor, I cannot let the women and children starve." The judge barked a few questions at Green and modified the injunction so that the union was allowed to feed the strikers.

Those years, besides unfolding a vista of complex experiences, also helped William Green, who had meanwhile become a member of the AFL's Executive Council, to build up a personal philosophy which, in later years, when he reached the pinnacle in labor leadership, served as a credo to guide his course of action. The grueling, bruising struggles of the miners with which he lived every hour of the day have not clouded William Green's vision or distorted his outlook. His belief that despite provocation his obligation as a citizen of a democracy comes first, both in thought and action, appears to have become strengthened with the years. "We endanger our freedom when we attempt direct action," he reiterated on many occasions, and he helped make this basic belief of his also the position of the UMW, although its membership, attuned to hourly physical dangers and harsh daily toil, gave way at times to impetuous action breaking through limits of endurance.

Time and again he asserted in those hectic years, in talks and by the written word, that the miners' battlefields were everywhere where coal was being mined, but that their contest was with the coal barons, not with the government or the country. But he just as vehemently protested the use or control of the government machinery by the coal operators for their own gain, and just as sharply condemned the issuance of injunctions and the employment of private armies by the mine owners.

Union Gospel to "New" Miners

During the nearly 35 years that William Green either worked in the mines or served as an officer of the miners' union, one of the complex problems the organized coal diggers had to meet was the constant influx of immigrants from all lands. The early miners were English, Welsh and Scotch, who came with an understanding of the traditions of unionism. As the reservoir of immigration moved eastward, and many immigrants who spoke no English and were wholly green to

American ways of living began pouring into the coal mines, the union became faced with the double responsibility of "housebreaking" this mass of new members to the rudiments of unionism, first in their own languages and later in teaching them English and adjusting them to the climate of a new land.

As the union's national secretary-treasurer, William Green for years directed these educational tasks, the issuing and distribution of union literature in several languages for these newcomers and the building up of cadres of organizers who could talk to them in their own tongues. The returns from this widespread educational work were invaluable from the UMW's viewpoint. The immigrants who entered the coal mines, after a few years of "acclimatization," proved to be a tower of strength in the union's future struggles for recognition and for higher living standards throughout the coal mining areas of the country. In speaking of these years of his officerhood in the United Mine Workers, William Green wrote: "Our union was an economic as well as a national institution. We believed then, as I believe now, that most men are honest, most of the time. . . . Along with other union representatives, I began to realize that in addition to organizing our economic power we would have to put some of our seasoned men into key political offices to secure the rights which citizens of a democracy should have."

Need for Labor Laws

Nowhere in the industrial precincts of the land was the helplessness of the individual worker more palpable than in a miner community and nowhere has the effort of unionism to replace the futility of individual effort by collective action been more urgent. As a young man William Green served on his local union's mine committee, which, among other duties, had the task of helping to take home miners who were badly hurt and the bodies of those who lost their lives in the frequent mine disasters. These mine committeemen also had to break the sad news to the stricken families.

"Many a time," Green wrote afterwards, "I have gone with aching

21

heart into a bare little shack to tell the wife that an accident had struck down her husband. I have seen the grief and the bravery of those women, knowing that there was not a dollar in the house for food or for the care of the small children. Usually, the pay was mortgaged ahead to the company store. The suffering I saw over the years made me resolve to work for a workmen's compensation system which at least would lighten the economic burden resulting from loss or disability of the family's breadwinner.

"In those years," Green continued, "pay-days came only once a month. Each month, as we lined up at the window for our pay, some member of the union would be standing there taking up a collection for John Jones or Bill Smith, or their wives and helpless children. The miners were always generous, but their pay was small and the demands for such collections too frequent to bring in sufficient sums. The injustice to us in the mining industry struck more forcibly because the accident rate was so high that a miner couldn't buy a dollar's worth of insurance from any company. When a miner was injured he usually got nothing as compensation. All the coal companies were insured by private insurance companies, and the insurance companies would fight each claim in the courts. They used all old common-law defenses, the doctrine of contributory negligence, the negligence of a fellow servant, and the known hazards of occupation. The miner had no chance. He was beaten practically before he started. The insurance companies won nearly every case."

Goal Set for Workmen's Compensation

Legislation was urgently needed, and, partly because of that, Bill Green consented to run for the Ohio Senate where he served from 1911 through 1913. As mentioned above, he succeeded in obtaining a majority for one important mine bill—the abolition of the mine-screen practice in the Ohio mines, but his chief legislative objective was to get a workmen's compensation law on the statute books. Green had at his command a huge volume of data at that time—he already was the

UMW's international statistician—and he had no difficulty in proving in support of his compensation bill that coal mining topped the list of industrial hazards and accidents in the country.

The insurance lobby, as anticipated, violently opposed the bill providing for a state insurance fund, but united labor behind the plan won Ohio's Governor Cox over for the bill's support. The evidence of injustice to the workers was so strong and the history of litigation over industrial injuries so disgraceful that public opinion was aroused and the law was adopted. When the Ohio law later was challenged by its opponents on the ground of constitutionality, one of the briefs filed in its defense was written by Louis D. Brandeis, already a valiant advocate of social legislation at that time, and later a noted liberal on the bench of the United States Supreme Court.

Health Insurance Next Target

The Ohio success proved infectious. In state after state other unions pushed the demands for workmen's compensation laws. William Green, inspired by the results, visited over a period of a dozen years many states and addressed labor and civic groups in support of workmen's compensation as an "object very dear to my heart," as he put it. Moreover, as a result of his successful campaign for a workmen's compensation law in Ohio, Green became convinced that disability and occupational ills should similarly be covered by legal provisions and there should be a general health insurance program.

He argued that the unions could give their members only limited insurance protection, but that responsibility for this protection rested upon society and so ultimately upon industry and the consumers who demanded the products of labor. Bitterly, William Green resented the fact that workers were not given at least as much consideration as a machine. Management must include in the cost of production the expense of repairs and replacement of worn parts of machinery, he argued. But when an employee becomes ill from causes arising out of his employment, the cost falls on the worker. The worker is bearing an industrial expense which should be borne by the industry.

In the second decade of this century, however, the leadership of the AFL was not ready to adopt this viewpoint in its entirety.

Opinion on socal health insurance for workers continued to be divided in the upper councils of the Federation for a number of years. Committees appointed by the Executive Council continued to hew to the line that compulsory health insurance, by and large, would not be helpful to the trade unions, subsequently conceding the point only that occupational diseases and injuries on the job be aided by legislation making industry financially responsible for that expense. They also stressed the urgency of expansion of union insurance programs.

William Green, however, continued to uphold the viewpoint of the minority that the loss of earning power was equally disastrous whether caused by injury or illness. The logical step after workmen's compensation, he argued, was a compulsory health insurance act. Only legislation, he asserted, would bring social justice here. Voluntary insurance, he contended, is out of reach for the low-wage family, and he flatly rejected the idea that compulsory insurance would mean the surrender of individual liberty of action.

"Poverty is the arch-enemy of freedom," Green insisted. "It is mockery to say to a sick worker whose family is in want that such a state of affairs should not be remedied by legislation because it might interfere with his 'personal rights' and 'liberty of action.'" Green had the solid support of the miners who had already taken a stand for compulsory health insurance. "We could trust the economic and political strength of unions to keep their essential rights inviolate under compulsory health insurance as under workmen's compensation," he summed up his position.

The differences between those who urged voluntary insurance and those who favored the compulsory system showed up in various resolutions at succeeding AFL conventions. In 1934, the convention of the Federation again approved a resolution to study health insurance. That year, President Green was appointed member of the Federal Economic Advisory Committee, which drafted a social insurance bill, including unemployment compensation and old-age benefits; health insurance, however, was not included in the social legislation measure which was finally enacted into law, falling far short of the committee's proposal, to Green's deep disappointment.

Medical Lobby Blocks Advance

Two years later, the 1936 convention of the Federation, after a study of costs of medical care, urged the federal government to create a commission that would study and recommend plans for an expanded system of social security to include medical care for sickness. At a conference representing all public groups, President William Green, speaking for all organized labor, offered his plan for extended workmen's compensation to cover illness and disease of all types, not only occupational in origin. This extension, covering workers' general health and their families, he proposed would include a measure of worker contributions to the general fund. One year later, at hearings before the Senate Committee on Labor, the Federation's spokesmen endorsed expansion of the public health program and enlargement of the social security system to include health insurance.

This action, marking a clear-cut departure from the old position of the Federation, was hailed by Green with extreme satisfaction. "It is a long time since I began working in Ohio, in 1916, for a social insurance program for workers. I expect to see social insurance extended to cover the hazards of general illness," he declared. William Green's optimistic expectations, however, still are a long way from realization. The coming of the war had shunted aside all extension of social security measures, while the postwar period, thus far, has witnessed an ultra-conservative trend away from social legislation. A powerful and heavily-financed medical lobby, besides, has succeeded in building up antagonism against national health insurance by presenting it as "socialized medicine," a barefaced and fraudulent bugaboo.

For the Nation's Children

William Green has worked with equal zeal for the protection of the nation's children, particularly for the prevention of the exploitation of the young in mine, mill and factory. The struggle to take the children away from the mines in the anthracite fields was begun at the turn of the century. The children, most of them orphans whose parents were lost in mine disasters, worked by the hundreds for a few pennies a day in the breakers, breathing the choking coal dust and working with cracked and bleeding fingers picking lumps of slate from the coal. The UMW wrote into its own laws a provision that no children under 16 be permitted to work in and around the mines. That, however, was only possible of enforcement in the strongly organized anthracite areas. "The wrong of child labor has always stirred me deeply," William Green commented in later years, "so this part of labor's program has been a personal matter with me."

From 1906 on, bills were introduced in Congress, year after year, to bar from interstate commerce the products of children under 14 years of age. One such bill, fixing penalties for violation, passed Congress in 1916. This was the Keating-Owen bill. It was, however, declared unconstitutional in June, 1918. Another law, the Pomerene Act, was passed by Congress and became a law in 1919, to be again declared unconstitutional.

The next step aimed at taking the youngsters out of mines and factories was offered by a large group of Congressmen and Senators from 14 states in the form of an amendment to the Constitution giving Congress the right to regulate the labor of children below 18 years of age. It passed both houses by huge majorities. A few states promptly ratified it. But rapidly a huge propaganda network was launched against it, and though the arguments against the amendment were flimsy and palpably false, they succeeded in turning away many people from support of child labor regulation.

In reporting the anti-child-labor amendment to the 1925 convention of the Federation, President William Green declared, amidst warm applause, "We have just begun to fight for the children of America. . . . We owe this opportunity for education and protection of their health to the citizens of the next generation."

Workers' Education in the AFL

In 1921, the Federation's convention voted to create a Committee on Education, first, to examine the systems and methods used in the public schools for civics, political economy and history, and, second, to promote adult education for workers. Subsequently, a Workers' Education Bureau, with a director and a staff, was organized by the Federation, chiefly for the promotion of adult education and for the publication of union literature. William Green took an active part in the work of this Education Committee as it proceeded to widen its program —to include support for a movement started in many states for the supply of free textbooks to children, and also to further labor representation on local boards of education and on boards of trustees of universities supported by public funds.

Green visualized the activity of the Committee on Workers' Education, from its beginning, as a sustained adult education movement among wage earners and as a preparatory phase for the wider participation of labor in all the civic and social functions of community and national life. He looked forward to the training of men and women who could present labor's case in legislatures and on administrative commissions. "We need the election of more labor men to legislatures," he emphasized, "and we need more labor men in responsible positions administering labor laws. . . . In my own two terms in the Ohio legislature I have introduced, in addition to several laws in favor of the miners, also a bill which limited the working hours of women to nine a day, which was passed. The public mind is much more receptive to such legislation now. It is all the more necessary to have our own people sharing in the framing of such laws."

Thus, William Green, while no protagonist of independent labor political parties, lined up firmly for the idea of political education among workers and for the election of labor men to state legislatures and on the national level. Unhesitatingly, and pointing to his own record in the Ohio Senate as he emerged fresh from the coal pits to take up political cudgels for his fellow miners, he welcomed labor's growing interest in politics as a means of defense or offense as arising situations required.

Shorter Workday for Women

In the early years, organized labor displayed no eagerness for supporting general legislation limiting working hours for men. It feared that such legislation might give the state too much power of regulation which would weaken the unions and hamper their own bargaining power to reduce the hours of labor. Unions, the argument ran, have by their own efforts brought down the workday in most lines of production. Women, however, were but poorly organized and their bargaining power was palpably weak.

In contrast to majority opinion, William Green, because of his experience in the Ohio Senate, showed no fear of fighting for shorter work hours by legislation. He was one of a minority group who voted back at the 1914 AFL convention in favor of making an effort to secure a general eight-hour law. President Gompers, however, sustained by a majority of delegates, opposed this move. Green, at that time secretary-treasurer of the UMW, accepted this defeat philosophically. Unions, he reasoned, are not inflexible in their policies. As economic and social conditions change, unions also are bound to alter their approach on how to meet new situations.

Many years later, with the enactment of the social legislation program of the New Deal in the 30's, which had the warm support of all organized labor, William Green's distant forecast of 1914 shaped up very much as a reality. The Fair Labor Standards Act met more than half way the issue raised earlier by the unions by fixing only minimum standards for the lowest paid wage earners by governmental regulation and leaving the unions free to negotiate through collective bargaining.

President Green's view regarding legislation affecting work hours and wages was summed up by him shortly after the Wage-Hour bill became law, in the following way: "Our attitude is no longer one of fear and distrust of government regulation under proper conditions. We welcome government efforts to provide on a social basis the security which it is not possible for a great proportion of men and women to achieve for themselves. We insist, however, that in the making and enforcing of this regulation labor shall have a fair part."

For Old-Age Pensions

Back in 1911, the Massachusetts State Federation of Labor introduced a resolution at the AFL convention putting the Federation on record in favor of a comprehensive national old-age pension system. Matters more pressing, however, had for years thereafter taken priority in AFL councils. Only in 1929, after an exhaustive study of old-age dependency, the AFL convention of that year heard a definite suggestion from its Executive Council of an active campaign for an adequate system of old-age pensions. Some of the delegates, however, felt even at that time that organized labor should concern itself exclusively with "perfecting its fighting organization," not with social legislation. William Green, from the chair, led in the support of this proposal, and the Federation went ahead with its agitation for this program.

Five years later, in 1934, President Green, as member of the Advisory Council on Economic Security, pledged the Federation's full support to national old-age provisions as part of the entire body of social legislation. No responsible group in the land, aside from inbred reactionaries, has since been able to refute the assertion that any legislation of the past half century has been of greater value to the general American community than the body of laws commonly described as the social security acts.

Jobless Benefits

Among the many problems darkening the industrial horizon and labor economics in particular, one of the most baffling had been the plague of unemployment which grew to immense size in the depression years 1929–33 and still remained a serious one even when prosperity returned in the early years of the Roosevelt administration.

William Green, together with most policy makers in organized labor, had looked askance at the outset at unemployment insurance fearing that a system of jobless benefits with the requirement that the claimant register and accept work offered through a public employment agency might result in forcing men to work under conditions which would jeopardize their union membership besides lowering earning standards. Unemployment should be solved by jobs not by insurance. The work hours in most industries, he was convinced, were far too long, and if the 30-hour week were generally accepted and enforced, the volume of unemployment would drastically recede, he contended.

President Green, together with the Executive Council, was, nevertheless, faced with the definitive failure of the national economy to provide work for all employables who were seeking jobs. He made a further study of this acute problem. The 1932 convention of the Federation finally accepted a resolution charging the Executive Council with promoting the passage of state unemployment compensation laws. Most of the leaders of the Federation were conscious that a national law would be preferable, but feared that such a law would be of doubtful constitutionality. Sentiment in favor of state laws thereupon grew rapidly and in 1933 bills were introduced in over half of the state legislatures. Congress also had before its consideration a number of proposals for a federal law.

The Advisory Council of the President's Committee on Economic Security, composed of citizens outside the government, at which Green was the leading spokesman for organized labor, gave the most serious thought to the relation of the federal and state governments in the insurance program, and the size of the tax and benefits. The Advisory Council recommended federal standards for benefits under a grant-in-aid provision rather than federal-state systems with credit offsets. President Green supported the Advisory Council, but the Committee for Economic Security favored the credit offset system.

"Unemployment a National Problem"

A half-dozen years later, Green wrote: "I am sure that the act will be extended and improved. . . . I believe that all our social security laws will ultimately have to be on a national scale. Industries extend across the continent. Labor in America is more mobile than in any other country in the world. Industries shift readily as we have seen in the migration of the boot and shoe industry westward and of cotton textiles to the South. In a society of fluid capital, migratory industries and shifting labor markets such as ours, unemployment is not a state problem and regulatory measures need to be national in scope."

In speaking of the AFL's continuing interest in the expansion of all forms of social security, Green added: "The spirit of pessimism does not prevail in the organized labor movement. Although our hopes have often been unrealized in respect to a particular piece of legislation or the reform of a patent evil, we continue to press our case by economic and political means at our disposal. . . . I know that organized labor will not fail to strive constantly for a better living for all mankind."

In World War I

William Green was a top officer in the UMW at the outbreak of World War I, though by the time America had entered that war, in April, 1917, he had already been a member of the AFL's Executive Council for nearly two years.

The coming of the war in Europe in 1914, which brought a munition production boom in this country and the rumblings of a preparedness campaign, had found the labor movement in no warlike mood. But when America entered the war in the spring of 1917, the unions stood ready to cooperate with the government in every way to win the war. Labor's first official act was the declaration at a nationwide conference of international unions, summoned by President Samuel Gompers, affirming American labor's allegiance to the government in peace and war, while stressing the maintenance of democratic procedures in the emergency. By accident, that conference and the declaration preceded by a few days the formal declaration of war.

A series of memoranda, or agreements, between the government and organized labor, signed by Newton D. Baker, then Secretary of War, and Samuel Gompers, accepted the union as the representative of its members, the union scales and working conditions of each locality, and set up joint adjustment boards on which the unions designated their representatives. This agreement covered construction work by the army and navy, shipbuilding and ship operations, the making of uniforms and other military equipment. The principle of labor representation, union recognition and collective bargaining appeared to be well accepted and became the policy of the War Labor Administrator. Labor was also given a place on all war labor agencies, including the National War Labor Board.

Nevertheless, the unions were eager, in William Green's words, "to re-establish at the end of the war, for the first time in many industries, a normal functioning relationship between employers and unions." Continued government control of labor relations, it was feared, might lead to government control of the unions and the death of an independent labor movement. In coal mining, the wartime experience of government intervention in labor relations was especially unfortunate. Despite their continued demands for wage increases to meet the rapidly rising cost of living, revision of wage scales was denied to the miners. The undertaking not to strike while the war lasted was another handicap which kept the miners' hands tied.

When the operators refused to consider the miners' demands in the spring of 1919 for cost-of-living pay increases, the union issued a strike call. An attempt to mediate by the Secretary of Labor having failed, President Wilson issued a statement demanding the recall of the strike order, and Attorney General Palmer asked for an injunction on the amazing ground that the wartime Lever Act still prohibited "profiteering in food and fuel." The ever-ready "injunction" Judge Anderson in Indianapolis promptly obliged with a sweeping writ, to which the miners replied with a complete stoppage of work.

Green Arrested

Eighty-four officers of the UMW, along with Secretary-Treasurer Green, were arrested for contempt of court, and after some legal pyrotechnics, Palmer asked the court to demand the withdrawal of the strike order. The request was complied with, but the miners still would not return to work. A month later, a commission, appointed by President Wilson, with the union's consent, to consider the wage question, granted a wage increase, but a much smaller one than the soft coal miners had asked. "This was not a happy ending to the mine workers' hopeful effort to work in every way possible with the government," Green caustically commented. The disastrous steel strike, led by William Z. Foster, shortly followed, and the mass offensive of industry against union organization thereafter was on its way.

The "open-shop" drive which gained full impetus after World War I was a bitter disappointment not only to the miners. The unions, which had proved during the war years that they were prepared to take their place in industry as well as in the trenches, had reason to hope, when the war ended, for a new friendly atmosphere in employer-labor relations in the huge non-union sectors in industry. This hope vanished when organized labor was suddenly confronted with the hard reality of an emerging and well-planned "open-shop" campaign sponsored by industry leaders. Company unions, under the high-sounding name of the "American Plan," were being started in almost every industry; professional strikebreakers, industrial spies, armed guards, company police, the blacklist, discharge for union activity were again brought into full play.

Labor's battle for the union shop and against the fraudulent, boss-owned unions, lasted until 1937, when the Wagner Act was finally upheld by the Supreme Court. Seven years before that, the nightmare of the injunction, which for a generation hung over the head of every union officer in the country, was lifted after the Norris-LaGuardia Act became law. In describing the injunction as it affected the daily activities of UMW, William Green tells that "many times it would become almost impossible for us to carry on our union affairs without violating an injunction. . . . We were often arrested, tried for contempt of court by the very judges who issued the injunctions. Since the courts had adopted the custom of issuing blanket injunctions covering 'all persons whomsoever,' it often happened that we violated court orders we knew nothing about. I believe that the use of the injunction in labor disputes has been one of the most serious perversions of justice in this country."

Presidency Brings New Tasks

William Green had a profound admiration for the Federation's founder. Samuel Gompers, Green often would say, understood and interpreted the spirit of the American workingman as no other man had ever succeeded in doing. And while Green occasionally disagreed with Gompers on labor and welfare legislation and on the best way of achieving it, by and large he clung to the "Old Chief's" trade-union ideology.

Voluntarism as the only true basis for democracy, in and out of the workshop, a doctrine which Gompers constantly preached and practiced, had served as the theme of his last message at the El Paso convention of the AFL, a message which, due to failing vision, Gompers felt he could not himself deliver, and which he asked William Green to read to the delegates. "I want to urge devotion to the fundamentals of human liberty," the message concluded, "the principles of voluntarism. No lasting gain has ever come from compulsion. If we seek force, we but tear apart that which, when united, is invincible."

William Green met his new tasks as presiding officer of the Federation with the same spiritual attributes and dogged courage which he displayed during the long years as local and later national mine union officer. He saw clearly the hurdles which were facing organized labor—the millions of unorganized workers in the mass production industries, the ever-growing army of women workers in the consumer industries, the almost untouched, huge reservoir of "white collar" workers in the offices and plants of the nation—and he was painfully eager to increase the membership of the Federation by converting these multitudes to trade unionism. Moreover, the new AFL president watched with tense concern the mounting torrent of anti-union propaganda which kept reviling organized labor by extolling the virtues of company unionism, the so-called American Plan.

34

"Mission to America"

To meet the challenge of the company union drive and its malevolent effect on public opinion, William Green, shortly after becoming president, undertook a one-man crusade to demonstrate—to industry and to the general public—the advantages of genuine trade unionism and to pierce, simultaneously, the inertia of the mass of non-union labor which remained apathetic to the call of union organization. Armed with inexhaustible persistence and an unswerving faith in the cause he was advocating, Green covered in the next half-dozen years some of the most important forums of the country—churchmen's conventions, schools of higher learning, chambers of commerce among them—preaching the gospel of organized labor.

He spoke at Harvard to a class of seniors at the School of Business Administration, and addressed audiences at Dartmouth and Columbia. Everywhere he emphasized the historic logic of the labor movement and stressed the point that modern conditions were calling for the wisdom of the conference table rather than settlement of labor disputes by "tactics of force." He emphatically rejected the theory that "differences between capital and labor are irreconcilable." Such a doctrine, Green argued, scorned the advances made by civilization and made a mockery of human progress. Organized labor, he said, was ready to replace the "might makes right" motto with a faith reflecting more modern ethics.

In 1925, the AFL, by convention approval, set up a new wage policy. This move, marking the second basic change in trade union wage policy since the start of the century, called for workers' real wages in the sense of purchasing power, coupled with a continued reduction in the number of hours making up the working day reflecting man's increasing power of production. This new policy was followed the next year, 1926, by the beginning of a drive for the forty-hour, five-day week.

In clarifying this policy, later in that year, in an address at Princeton University, Green made it clear that he was interested not merely in promoting harmony between industry and labor but in increasing

35

facing slow starvation, were losing their grip on self-reliance and were driven into dependency. Thus the witches' cauldron of speculation was boiling over while the unwary public took the foam of the speculator's brew to be tangible wealth.

William Green, who felt keenly the urgency of a solution to the devastating unemployment problem beyond the palliative of temporary relief, realized likewise that it was beyond the power of any individual group to provide a realistic answer to the grievous situation which involved deeply-rooted social, industrial and monetary factors. It became clear to him, and he vigorously expressed this thought from convention platforms and at public meetings, that the hour called for a drastic and joint effort by all organized national groups and bodies to stem the crisis.

In April, 1930, President Green offered to the Senate Committee on Commerce, on behalf of the Executive Council, a five-point plan which included, besides periodic censuses of unemployment, the training and retraining of workers made jobless by technological changes, a nationwide employment service, a permanent program of public works in periods of depression, and a proposal for a simultaneous cut in working hours in all industries, with the maintenance of the same weekly pay. The AFL program, however, received but slight support from the various Congressional committees which had to deal with the grievous unemployment situation, and Green's repeated appeals to President Hoover to call a national economic conference to take drastic measures for halting the snowballing economic paralysis had no effect.

NRA, Wagner Act

At the annual AFL convention, in November, 1932, however, with Franklin D. Roosevelt already elected along with a new Congress, President Green appealed to the delegates to sanction a proposal for a five-day work-week and six-hour workday by statute. Green put the issue squarely to the convention: either the country's industry is to be completely dismantled and wiped out, or some effective and far-reaching adjustments must be made. The convention, without a single dissenting vote, approved the step. President Green thereupon submitted to the new Congress early in 1933 the 30-hour-week plan as a "basis for economic recovery."

A bill for a 30-hour week passed the Senate in the spring of 1933, but a legislative compromise meanwhile had been worked out and embodied in a substitute measure combining a number of labor proposals with the program framed by the Roosevelt administration. That measure was the National Recovery Act.

The New Deal program was a conscious effort to restore to the American workingman the rights and the prerogatives to which he was entitled as a citizen but which Congress and the courts had whittled away over a great many years by legislation and judicial interpretation. With the injunction already curbed a year before by the Norris-LaGuardia Act, the new Congress proceeded to establish the right of labor to organize in the famous Section 7(A) of the Recovery Act which, in explicit terms, guaranteed to all "employees the right to organize and bargain collectively through representatives of their own choosing, and shall be free from interference, restraint, or coercion by employers of labor, or their agents, in the designation of such representatives or in self-organization or in other concerted activities for the purpose of collective bargaining or other mutual aid or protection." Section 7(A) also provided that no workers, employed or seeking employment, shall be required as a condition of employment to join any company union.

Under the Recovery Act, which went into effect on June 16, 1933, it is true, labor was given no direct participation in the formulation of minimum wage and maximum hour standards. Even so, under the initial re-employment agreements promulgated under the NRA and under the subsequent codes, a vast program was achieved. But in the spring of 1935, the Supreme Court declared the NRA unconstitutional, and before the year was out a survey made by the AFL revealed that as a direct result of the abandonment of the maximum hours rule, more than 1,800,000 were again deprived of their jobs.

Within a few months, however, the Wagner Act, into which the contents of Section 7(A) of the NRA were incorporated, became law. The Wagner Act was promulgated as an extension of the "commerce and general welfare" clauses of the Constitution to safeguard it from adverse interpretation by the Supreme Court. The new act established the right of collective bargaining and majority rule in all industrial plants in unmistakably clear terms; it defined unfair labor practices, and provided a simple method of enforcing the law. Organized labor hailed it as its "Magna Charta," a law that placed labor on a plane of equality with industry within the social framework of the nation.

The Wage-Hour Act

While continuing to press for the 30-hour bill, the AFL, under the direction of President Green, was faced with resurgent opposition by reactionary employer groups, which had become encouraged by the invalidation of the NRA, to any minimum-wage and maximum-hour legislation.

The Fair Labor Standards Law, finally adopted as a satisfactory compromise, was based on the principle of a gradual reduction of weekly hours of work and gradual increase of minimum wage rates, affecting the total readjustment over a running period of years. Applying only to employers operating in interstate commerce, it affected some 11 million workers in the low-wage levels at the time of its enactment.

Over the years, however, the range of the new act, better known as the Wage-Hour Law, has expanded to take in more millions and its minimum wage rates have made healthy climbs, from the original 40 cents per hour to a 70-cent minimum. It is regarded as one of the most beneficial and enduring labor acts passed during the New Deal era.

The New Union Sweep

The new labor laws gave the trade union movement a powerful spurt. Millions of unorganized workers became actively interested in union affiliation. Optimism in the trade union world ran so high that at the 1933 convention of the Federation, enthusiastic predictions visu-

40

alized an early membership potential of 25 million. To be sure, a great many die-hard employers continued to fight desperately against the unionization of their workers, but they clearly were waging a losing battle. By the time the Wagner Act was approved by the Supreme Court in 1937, the union movement had more than doubled its membership; and this notable increase, it may be noted, came about despite acute discord and disunion within the national labor family.

Throughout that period of high hopes and accelerated activity on all fronts, President Green, with the full support and encouragement of the Executive Council and the unceasing endorsements of AFL conventions, had kept up a drive for the adoption of an accelerated national program of security through unemployment benefits, old-age benefits and public assistance for maternal and child welfare. He advocated with equal fervor a national health insurance plan. He fought for the adoption of a low-rent housing and slum-clearing program, the program subsequently embodied in the U.S. Housing Act. He continued hammering for the support of a long-range program of permanent public works which would provide public channels for private investments in periods of depression.

In step with his steadfast philosophy of mutuality of interests among all groups in the national life, Green constantly gave full expression to the thought that he wanted a "joint cooperative endeavor on the part of all representative groups to plan for the future, analyze trends and conditions and devise methods for bringing new and more equitable balance in the country's economic relationships."

Men—and Policies

In retrospect, it may be observed that during these years of trade union upsweep in the 30's, as in the preceding years of ebbtide and hard-pulling against a stonewall of employer antagonism, William Green carried on his presidency job with unflinching dignity, treating obstacles and roadblocks as passing deterrents only.

There had been divided opinion in those hectic years also in the AFL's top executive group—sharp jurisdictional disputes, disagreements on the use of political pressures, varying outlooks on cooperation with labor abroad, and differing attitudes on labor and social legislation. The espousal of conflicting policies involved such pillars on the Executive Council as William L. Hutcheson, indomitable president of the Carpenters' Brotherhood from 1915 to 1951, Daniel J. Tobin, forceful chieftain of the Teamsters' Brotherhood, largest single AFL union, George M. Harrison, affable president of the Railway Clerks, Matthew Woll, custodian of AFL philosophy and front-rank fighter for world free labor, David Dubinsky, dynamic leader of the Ladies' Garment Workers, and Harry C. Bates, head of the Bricklayers and Masons and a key figure in the building trades.

William Green, it is fair to state, has owned no magic formula for resolving all recurring conflicts of opinion on internal as well as external policy, but he has had one sure compass to guide him—a firm resolution to keep the AFL functioning and to preserve intact the great family of organized workers to which he is emotionally tied by a million strings. In this, beyond cavil, he has succeeded eminently. And it is also fair to state that through the years the leading figures of the Executive Council, regardless of their personal views, have given him consistently loyal support.

On the Eve of World War II

While Hitler's drive for world domination began unfolding itself in the mid-30's, America, under the pressure of dominant pacifist strains of public opinion passed a "Neutrality Act" in the hope of steering clear of war involvements. In major outlines, the escapist state of mind of that period followed the pattern of the first two years of World War I, when Woodrow Wilson was re-elected in 1916 with the aid of the "he-kept-us-out-of-war" slogan.

Speaking for the body of organized labor, as late as May, 1939, William Green was saying, "American labor wants peace, not war . . . We, therefore, ask that the present Neutrality Act be continued in effect. We are not insensitive to the struggle that is going on in this world, but in the light of World War experience, we hold that war settles nothing and that future generations should not be asked to serve in the trenches." And when, upon the invasion of Poland, England and France entered the war against the Nazis, he still held that "labor firmly believes that we should have no part in this European war . . . We want policies best calculated to keep us free of European entanglements."

"Geography Is No Security"

That state of mind, insofar as the organized workers of the country were concerned, however, did not last long. The surge of the Nazi armies across the European continent, the conquest of Norway and Denmark, the Dunkirk epic, and the virtual siege of Britain quickly swept complacency out of the minds and hearts of the American people. Roosevelt's vigorous national defense program was hailed by the AFL's Executive Council in a statement declaring that the labor movement is "solidly and squarely behind the President in national preparedness to advance and defend American ideals of life," warning, however, that in defense production there shall be no lowering or suspension of labor standards. In an editorial in the "American Federationist," President Green declared that "Geography provides no security from the destruction that stalks Europe."

Loathing the Hitler-Stalin pact, which gave the Nazis the green light for the invasion of Poland and led subsequently to the butchery of millions of non-combatants by Hitler's blood-soaked "supermen," William Green, at a great public dinner in his honor on June 26, 1940, at the Hotel Commodore in New York, declared that the democracies of Europe had, in a measure, invited their own destruction at the hands of Hitler's armies because they had watched in cold blood and without lifting a protesting voice the ruthless destruction of the Jewish population of Germany only a few years before.

"As we look back now we see clearly that the democracies of Europe might have saved themselves if they had said to Hitler at the moment he started his first anti-Semitic purges: 'Stop! We will not permit such inhuman persecution. It is a menace to our civilization and a disgrace to the world.' " Green said, adding, "There is another lesson we must not forget and that is that Hitler, Stalin and Mussolini are partners in international crime and that Nazism, Communism and Fascism are but different labels for the same system of totalitarianism."

Four-Square on Defense

By the summer of 1940, the defense effort was in full swing, with plants converting rapidly for the production of armaments as President Roosevelt was signing the nation's first peacetime draft bill. Early in 1941, President Green declared, "To date, there has not been a single strike that has impeded the defense program, and it must be borne in mind that wars of today are determined largely in the shops and by the ability to maintain supplies." He, however, expressed some worry over "danger of defense production workers being stranded in munition areas or in industries expanded for defense production" who might be sucked into a vacuum of unemployment unless sane and practical channels of civilian re-employment were given deliberate thought in advance.

Events moved rapidly from that point to a climax. The enactment of "Lend Lease" was followed in the spring of 1941 by President Roosevelt's proclamation of unlimited national emergency, and speaking for the AFL, President Green greeted it with a statement that "we are in a world struggle, and we shall be vitally affected by the outcome of this struggle, which cannot be decided without our aid."

Clear-Headed on Domestic Reds

In June, 1941, Hitler invaded his erstwhile ally, Soviet Russia. Millions of Americans who had as little use for Stalin as they had for Hitler were suddenly faced with a weird world situation which, willy-nilly, projected Stalin's oligarchy as our ally in the fight to destroy Hitler. An ironic by-play of that moment also was the sudden conversion of the domestic Stalin stooges, who had until then denounced the American preparedness program as a "betrayal of the cause of world

44

peace," to a fervid endorsement of Lend Lease, of unlimited aid to Britain, France and, of course, to Soviet Russia.

Only one sector, and a very important one, of the general community appeared to have kept its head clear on this sudden Communist somersault. In a ringing editorial in the "American Federationist" of July, 1941, William Green wrote: "The right-about-face of the Communist Party since the Nazis invaded Russia constitutes no reason for us to alter our attitude towards them. Communists' support of the defense program in order to aid the Soviet Union does not remove the reasons why labor fights them as deadly enemies. In this time of worldwide peril to the cause of worldwide freedom, it is fitting for a revival of unionism and individual determination to put the cause of human freedom above all other considerations." And again: "The whole nation depends on the unions to maintain Americanism on the labor front; it is essential, therefore, that no Communist be permitted to act as an officer of any union affiliated with the AFL."

Strikes "Out for Duration"

Immediately after America entered the war, the AFL solemnly declared that "strikes are out for the duration," and this pledge, with but minor lapses, was faithfully observed to the last day of hostilities. "This is American labor's war," William Green emphatically stated, "and our strike record, I am convinced, will prove an example of what free men, with an indomitable will to win, will do voluntarily for their country."

While labor's record during the war served to accentuate the staunch loyalty of America's wage earners in the defense of their homeland's ways of living, it failed to impress many domineering industry leaders who even during the war refused to abandon or shelve hostility to the unions. Already, a few months after the country became involved in the global fight, in April, 1942, sniping at labor was started in Congress and in some sections of the press largely because the AFL was demanding effective price control and also protection for small business in armament production. While the war lasted, however, anti-labor bills introduced in Congress were pigeonholed and critical situations were avoided. Perhaps the finest tribute paid to labor during the entire conflict was the statement issued in March, 1944, by the War Investigating Committee (the Truman Committee) in speaking of the manpower factor contributed by labor: "This astounding performance —the rise of 76% over the 1939 record—exceeds anything of its kind ever achieved in the history of the world. The results are the best answer to the critics of the home front."

Postwar Era in Offing

As the war was drawing to a close, the labor movement, for the second time in a generation, began casting its eyes toward the oncoming postwar period and its tortuous aftermath. Veterans' re-employment, reconversion, postwar wages, the re-entrance of fighting men into the climate of a world again at peace, and not the least—the question of labor's share in peacemaking—were churning rapidly in the minds of labor's leadership. The AFL, speaking through the voice of William Green, was demanding a place for labor at the forthcoming peace conferences. "In asking for representation in the making of peace, labor is simply asking for service, not special privilege."

On April 12, 1945, the unexpected death of Franklin Delano Roosevelt shocked the nation. In Europe the war was nearing its fateful end, but in the Pacific the final stages of the conflict still demanded huge sacrifices. William Green, in commenting on the demise of FDR, said: "His death constitutes a heavy loss to every wage earner in the nation . . . It is a heavy loss also to the entire freedom-loving world . . . Our new President, Harry S. Truman, is ideally fitted by nature and experience to carry on. An able and sincere man, he can and will unite America not only by consummation of military victory but for the inauguration of a postwar program of enduring peace and domestic prosperity."

William Green's hopes for domestic prosperity following the war were largely realized. His prophecy, or, rather, hope that President Truman would unite the country behind him in an effort for domestic

46

progress, however, was toppled by the fierce partisanship of reactionary politicos and industrial tycoons whose hate of his Fair Deal policies was only exceeded by their hunger for power. Nor have the past seven years since the war came to an end given the world even a glimmer of hope for an enduring peace.

Taft-Hartley Arrives

By the time the Wagner Act reached its tenth anniversary, in June, 1945, organized labor realized that a solid bloc of anti-labor Congressmen and Senators, with Senator Robert A. Taft of Ohio as its chief brain-truster, was planning to scuttle, or emasculate organized labor's "Magna Charta" and to substitute for it a law that would shear the unions of their position of relative equality in their relations with employers.

Their worst fears soon were realized when the Old Guard Republicans, capitalizing on the country's postwar weariness, captured in the 1946 elections both houses of Congress and, within a few months, passed the Taft-Hartley Industrial Disputes Act, which made a shambles of the Wagner Act and revived labor's memories of company cops, lockouts, broken strikes and ex-parte injunctions. Stripped of verbiage, the Taft-Hartley Act deprived the unions of the closed shop, its choicest guarantee of union shop security, and outlawed as "secondary boycott" the refusal on the part of union labor to handle struck-shop or non-union products, a formidable economic weapon against strike-breaking by indirection. In legalizing injunctions against unions under a variety of conditions, virtually outlawed for 15 years by the Norris-LaGuardia Act, the Taft-Hartley Act again made unions vulnerable to court actions.

This barefaced hostility of the 80th Congress to organized labor aroused William Green to a fighting pitch. When the Taft-Hartley bills were first introduced, the AFL president, in testimony before Congressional committees and in numerous speeches and articles, inveighed against the proposed law with evangelical fervor, as a "piece of vicious anti-union legislation." Green sparked the fight against the proposed

47

act, engaging in two radio debates, one with Senator Taft and another with Earl Bunting, then president of the National Manufacturers Association. Together with New York's former Governor, now United States Senator, Herbert H. Lehman, AFL Secretary-Treasurer George Meany, and ILGWU President David Dubinsky, he addressed a great Madison Square Garden "veto" meeting in New York at which President Truman was exhorted to veto the anti-union act if it were passed. When the Taft-Hartley Act was passed over President Truman's veto, President Green declared that the Federation would at once begin a campaign for its repeal.

LLPE—New Political Arm

In a sense, the adoption of the Taft-Hartley Act has served to create a focal point of new political awareness throughout the Federation. At its 1947 convention, at San Francisco, the anti-labor law spawned by "Mr. Republican," a tag Senator Taft is particularly fond of, became a central theme on the convention's agenda. Without a dissenting vote, the delegates voted to organize Labor's League for Political Education, to be financed by contributions of individual trade unionists—the Taft-Hartley Act forbade contributions from union funds for political activity on the federal level—to strengthen and to coordinate the fight against political candidates hostile to organized labor. While the Federation has for more than 50 years adhered to a policy of "rewarding friends and punishing enemies of labor," the ways and means for carrying out that strategy, however, had in the past been rather loose and lacked coordination.

Labor's League for Political Education, known as LLPE, has since gone through two Congressional campaigns, and is currently getting ready for the 1952 election. It is organized as a nationwide network and functions throughout the year, equipped with a staff of experienced political workers and using the airwaves as well as television to deliver its message. While its immediate or concrete results to date have been moderate, its value as a political educational instrument is rated quite highly. It has brought the urgency of labor politics into hundreds of thousands of workers' homes where political awareness was lacking before.

Cold War Finds Labor Alerted

The national emergency created by the cold war, the draft which pulled out hundreds of thousands of young men from the factories only a short few years after millions of their older brothers had been demobilized, found the trade union movement this time fully alerted to the gravity of the emerging world crisis. The Kremlin was making a mockery of every pledge of peaceful behavior it had made to its war allies and was getting ready to sink its fangs deeper into the weakened body of Western Europe.

Speaking of the European Recovery Program, promulgated by President Truman in the spring of 1948, President Green commented, "The basic purpose of this comprehensive relief move, as labor understands it, is to enable European nations to restore the economic foundations which maintained the European way of life characterized by human rights and freedom." Later, in June, 1949, he greeted the Atlantic Pact as "representing a definite change in U. S. policy" but accepting it as an imperative necessity as "the time has come when democratic nations must act together for the protection of their liberties."

This endorsement of the government's foreign policy by the AFL and its wholehearted support to the national rearmament drive, has not blinded its eyes to the urgency of watchful vigilance over both policy and practices connected with the defense mobilization program. With the experience of the early 40's fresh in mind, when industry's "dollar-a-year-men" swarmed all government policy and production war agencies with organized labor reduced, not too politely, to areas of timid observation, the AFL—working in unison with the CIO and other independent unions—formed in the summer of 1950 a "United Labor Policy Committee." The unions had been given some minor places in the defense outfit with but meagre voices on the advisory level, and the new labor committee undertook a drive to secure a stronger position for labor spokesmen, chiefly in the price and wage stabilization sectors of the program.

Having met with rebuffs from the top command at the Defense Mobilization Office and with but little sympathy in Congress, the United Labor Policy Committee, in a dramatic move, withdrew in February, 1951, all labor representatives serving on the mobilization agencies. Declaring itself "thoroughly disillusioned" with the attitude of the powers-that-be in the defense program, the United Labor Policy Committee declared that it "regrets that to date labor has not enjoyed opportunity for full participation in the mobilization effort." Foreshadowing this decision, President Green, in a public statement following the declaration by President Truman of a national emergency in January, 1951, declared that "no functional group has a monopoly of industrial experience . . . Teamwork, the distinctively American practice, gives the best results . . . In this period of emergency, we urge unlimited use of teamwork."

Equal Sacrifice a "Must" for All

On March 21, 1951, a meeting of 700 union leaders, summoned by the United Labor Policy Committee, met in Washington and demanded a new Defense Production Act to supplant what it termed the "Big Business" show which was running defense mobilization all the way down the line. President Green and Secretary-Treasurer Meany both emphasized at that meeting that "the combined segments of the American labor community call for 'equality of sacrifice' which the present emergency requires from all Americans." Both AFL leaders denounced exorbitant rents and spiraling prices without rigid controls to hold in check lust for profits, and "the larding of the Production Act with special privileges for business interests."

The United Labor Policy Committee later met with President Truman and agreed to join a National Advisory Board on Mobilization Policy. Some substantial administrative reshuffling was subsequently effected which gave representatives from both the AFL and the CIO some key spots in the mobilization outfit. The 82nd Congress, like its predecessor, the 81st Congress, largely dominated by business-dedicated Republican tories and Dixiecrats, however, stuck to its anti-labor guns and "to-hell-with-the-consumer" attitudes.

Grappling With the Red Hydra

The desperate and protracted fight which the American trade unions had had to wage in the years following World War I against the "open shop" drive, an outright effort to crush legitimate trade unionism by substitution of employer-dominated groups, became even more complicated in the early 20's by an insidious crusade from the "left," the Communist campaign to invade and capture AFL unions and, ultimately, to gain thereby control of the American labor movement.

In discussing early Communist infiltration moves, William Green later wrote that the attempts of the Red agents to gain a foothold among the miners, one of their first infiltration efforts, were never successful. Only in Nova Scotia did they gain any strength but that attempt soon petered out after the Nova Scotia charter was withdrawn for failure to obey international union orders. In a number of other unions, however, the Communist boring policy met with much greater success. For a time they appeared to gain supremacy in the garment trades, in furs and in some transport unions. They were ultimately defeated by the ILGWU, but not before they had caused almost irreparable harm to that union. In the Fur Workers' Union, unfortunately, they remained in control, with the result that it has lost much of its strength in New York, its chief market.

"When the Communists launched their campaign to gain control of the AFL," Green continued, "we were not unfamiliar with such previous disruptive attempts. During the period when the IWW had been active, it had also made efforts to destroy or control established unions within the Federation . . . The IWW, however, had never been a serious threat, and during the war its strength steadily declined. The Communists, however, became a greater menace to the AFL than the IWW had ever been because of their stealthy, conspiratory tactics to gain control of our unions by 'boring from within.' "

51

No "Freedom of Choice"

In the first years of the Soviet rule in Russia, William Green, along with many other leaders of labor and liberal-minded Americans, had been inclined to the viewpoint that while Communist activities in America were disruptive and destructive and had to be combated at every step and turn, the "Russian workers should be left free from all outside interference in their choice of the economic and political systems under which they choose to live." This judgment, however, has undergone a drastic change. The stark revelation of the total absence of any "freedom of choice" in either economic or political matters to Soviet inhabitants; of the millions enslaved in the "corrective" labor camps in the Soviet domain; the Stalin-Hitler pact of 1939, and all the subsequent acts of international perfidy and fraud committed by the Kremlin, have long since opened the eyes of practically all Americans to the overriding urgency of a defensive alliance of all freedom-loving peoples against the menace of world Communism.

In this alliance, the oppressed and helpless peoples of the Soviet empire obviously cannot be classed as disinterested "free agents" who need no help or "interference" in determining their own destinies.

The CIO—and "Labor Peace"

A dramatic point in American labor history was reached in the formation of the "Committee for Industrial Organization" following turbulent debates at the 1935 AFL convention in Atlantic City. Piloted by John L. Lewis, president of the United Mine Workers, this committee, set up originally to promote unionization in the mass production industries outside regular AFL organizational channels, three years later became the Congress of Industrial Organizations (CIO), a full-fledged rival central body to the AFL.

Lewis was joined in this move by a half-dozen other unions whose leadership advocated more aggressive organization in the mass production industries, notably in autos, steel, rubber, oil and communications. A number of these unions, however, which never contemplated dual unionism, returned to the AFL after the Committee for Industrial Organization became the Congress of Industrial Organizations at its Pittsburgh convention in the fall of 1938.

To William Green the defection of Lewis and of the United Mine Workers in particular had come as a grievous shock in which the personal element was not lacking. The Mine Workers had been union home to Green, an emotional center with which fifty years of his life had been bound up. The break also came at a time when, in William Green's words, the AFL was gathering strength and resources for a full-fledged attack in the very same areas toward which the Lewis movement announced it was heading. The Lewis viewpoint at that 1935 convention, besides, had been heavily outvoted both in committee and on the convention floor. By every standard, therefore, Green regarded the Lewis-inspired defection as an open violation of democratic procedure and a flagrant revolt against the supreme authority of the AFL, its annual convention.

Green resented even more strongly the effort of Lewis to split the convention and public opinion on what, he asserted, was the unreal and spurious issue of industrial versus craft unionism. Having been brought up in a militant industrial union, where every man in and around the mines belonged to the same local regardless of skill, Green refused to accept the logic of division within the trade union movement on craft versus industrial lines. Within the AFL itself there were at that time—and have since been—autonomous industrial, semi-industrial, as well as craft unions. Green bitterly assailed Lewis as a man "consumed with personal ambition who gave the lie to the democratic process after it had rejected his leadership."

The history of the following dozen years covering relations between the AFL and the CIO need not be recited here—it is too well known generally, for one thing, and this limited space forbids it. Green's original reaction to the CIO and to John Lewis, however, has stood up well through the run of years. By now, as the bitter animosity of the early days in both camps has subsided considerably, it has become quite clear that the craft-industrial issue lies dead and buried. William

Green's appraisal of Lewis appears to have been amply justified by succeeding events. After seven years of what seemed to be unchallenged CIO leadership, Lewis had been forced to leave it in a mood of frustration, yielding his post to an officer who for many years had been his second in command in the United Mine Workers. A few years later he re-entered the AFL, remaining in it for one year and departing again in a huff because an overwhelming majority of the 1947 convention of the AFL refused to go along with him on the question of signing anti-Communist affidavits.

"No Substitute for Organic Unity"

During the last war, the AFL and the CIO cooperated frequently both on national and local levels in keeping the country's industrial machine at a high tempo. With the passing of the Taft-Hartley Act, CIO and AFL committees in many districts have worked together politically to help defeat some of labor's most outspoken enemies. The Communist invasion of South Korea and the ensuing preparedness drive which has put the country on a semi-war footing industrially, brought into being early in 1951 a "United Labor Policy Committee," formed for the avowed purpose of strengthening labor's influence in the government's mobilization agencies.

As told elsewhere here, this ULPC was dissolved one year later, without too much audible rancor. Its dissolution caused some chagrin among those who had expected that the ULPC was a definitive forerunner of labor unity. From the AFL came the explanation that the committee's usefulness had come to an end after it served the purpose for which it was created. The AFL said the next step in united labor action, if it is ever to materialize, should be organic unity, an all-embracing merger which the AFL has been supporting since labor peace talks started in 1937. In "Federationist" editorials and in recent public statements, President Green has ascribed the CIO's disinclination to discuss seriously a labor merger to fear of being overwhelmed by a numerically much stronger partner. This, however, he declared, is an unrealistic attitude. "Trade unionists do mix, and it is more likely that

54

the CIO unions would exercise more influence in a united organization than their present numerical strength would indicate," he asserted. On the other hand, organic unity would be of great help to labor on a national scale. "Organized labor's stock is at a low ebb in Congress, and many other groups wield far more influence," Green went on to say. But temporary committees and makeshifts can hardly be expected to achieve basic results. "There is no substitute for organic unity in the labor movement, there can be none," and the AFL president is convinced that there are no obstacles to organic unity that cannot be overcome given a climate of honest give-and-take and of fundamental good will.

"Hands Across Seas" 60 Years Old

AFL contacts with organized labor abroad began in 1894 when the fledgling federation voted for a regular exchange of convention delegates with the British Trades Union Congress, an exchange it has faithfully adhered to for nearly 60 years. Eighteen years later, in 1912, the AFL joined the National Trade Union Centers, an organization formed by the German and Scandinavian trade unions, which was seeking affiliates in Europe and other continents. This body failed to meet the severe tests of labor fraternity during World War I and it fell apart. In 1919, however, it was reorganized as the International Federation of Trade Unions.

For a number of years the AFL declined to accept membership in the IFTU because the new body would not undertake to respect the autonomy of affiliated national trade union movements. Only after the AFL had obtained the explicit guarantee that the American trade union center was sovereign in its own affairs did it join the IFTU in the middle 1930's. With the rise of totalitarian states in Europe—in Soviet Russia, Nazi Germany and in Fascist Italy—their state-controlled unions sought on several occasions admission into the IFTU, but were rejected. During World War II, after Hitler had cast his treaty with Stalin out the window and invaded Russia, the AFL was asked to join an Anglo-Soviet Commission. The AFL declined the invitation stating that it could not compromise on principle. In his reply, President Green bluntly declared, "We have common war objectives with Soviet Russia, that's true, but our objectives for world peace and labor welfare in general are not identical."

"No Truck With Red Unions"

The then general secretary of the British Trades Union Congress, Walter Citrine, thereupon decided to ignore the existing IFTU and issued a call for a "world labor conference," inviting all organizations from each country to meet in London, including Soviet state-run unions. The AFL again rejected the invitation to that conference which took place in October 1945. "Free trade unions," President Green for a second time explained in an editorial in the "Federationist," "cannot work together with state-controlled unions . . . Soviet union officers must be approved by trusted representatives of their Communist Party. They are not free to negotiate their wages and conditions of work. Infractions of work rules, failure to produce as expected, tardiness send thousands of Russian workers to 'corrective' camps. It is estimated that the number of persons in these man-devouring penal camps fluctuates between 12 and 20 millions."

Yet, while refusing to line up with the so-called World Federation of Trade Unions, the AFL leadership kept its sights high upon the international labor scene in the Western Hemisphere, in Europe and in other world pivotal centers. This intense fraternity with free labor everywhere, in countries where it had been weakened by the last war or had ceased to exist owing to ruthless repression by totalitarian regimes, has in the past few years become a functional part of the AFL, growing in depth and in volume and supplying a highly satisfying spiritual content throughout the Federation. This story of what labor, and the AFL in particular, has been doing in the international field in this gravest of world crises which has now lasted for nearly twelve years obviously cannot be told in full in this brief biography of William Green.

It is patent, nevertheless, as George Meany, AFL secretary-treasurer, remarked in a recent public address, that "without the full and energetic support of our organized labor movement, neither America nor the labor organizations of other countries can halt—let alone smash —the nefarious Communist conspiracy for world domination by Soviet Russia."

New Ties With Free Labor

The time-tested consistency of the AFL in its refusal to affiliate with any world labor center which admits Communists or their stooges, paid off in moral dividends when in November, 1949, the British Trades Union Congress, the American CIO and several other free unions, after withdrawing from the World Federation of Trade Unions earlier that year, met in London and formed, together with the AFL, the International Confederation of Free Trade Unions. The new world labor body, which admits no state-controlled unions, represented at its founding meeting 47 million workers from 50 countries. It set up international headquarters at Brussels, Belgium.

The AFL delegates at the London conference included President William Green, Secretary-Treasurer George Meany, and five of its vice presidents—Matthew Woll, George M. Harrison, W. C. Doherty, David Dubinsky and Charles J. McGowan—as well as George P. Delaney, AFL international representative, and Irving Brown and Henry Rutz, AFL representatives in Europe. In addressing the delegates at the end of the conference, President Green, among other things, said: "We have learned out of our war experience, revolution and counter-revolution that only the maximum cooperation of the forces devoted to human freedom and social and economic justice can preserve liberty, freedom and justice. That is why we want a strong, militant, fighting international confederation of free trade unions. We are ready to give our all to such a movement. But the greatest contribution American labor can make to this movement is in the moral and spiritual sense rather than in the material. Our undying hatred of every form of slavery and despotism is the greatest contribution we can make. Our unstinting devotion to human freedom and social justice is a most *price-less* asset of international labor solidarity."

The second World Congress of the ICFTU was held early in July, 1951, in Milan, Italy. It was attended by delegates from 55 countries representing $52\frac{1}{2}$ million workers. Since that Congress, the Australian Council of Trade Unions and several other national groups have been accepted for membership and in 1952 the ICFTU had a combined membership of $53\frac{1}{2}$ million.

ICFTU Comes to Latin America

Another highly significant phase of AFL world labor relations touched upon with considerable elation by President Green is cooperation with the free labor movements in Latin America. He stressed especially Secretary Meany's leadership and initiative in this field of action. The fight for free trade unionism in Latin America is also a fight for elementary civil rights and the conflict is made even harder by the unholy combination of Communists and Peronist totalitarians who are seeking to block free trade unionism not only in Argentina but throughout South America.

The hard work of the past half-dozen years, however, is yielding results. Only a short time ago the pro-Communist labor padrone, Lombardo Toledano, was regarded as the undisputed dictator of Latin American workers. Today his power is at a vanishing point. His erstwhile well-oiled machine is grinding to a stop in most countries in Latin America, and this Communist decline has come chiefly through the driving initiative of the AFL which in January, 1951, succeeded in founding an Inter-American Regional Organization of the ICFTU. This regional body embraces not only the AFL but the CIO and the two central labor bodies of Canada. Serafino Romualdi, who has served indefatigably for the past ten years as the AFL's Latin American field representative, contributed substantially toward the formation of this regional free labor center.

Secretary Meany, who took a leading part in the formation of the ORIT, as the regional Latin American group is better known, in describing its aims, said: "Our main task all these years has been to help the workers of our sister American Republics in their struggles to secure a higher standard of living and to defend freedom of trade union organization." He referred to the attempts of some Peronista agents to sneak into the Regional Organization in the following words: "The henchmen of the Argentine dictator were even so bold as to make an open attempt to join our fold. But we place principles above power politics and we kept these totalitarian termites out of our all-American house of labor."

AFL's "Foreign Office" at Work

As AFL contacts with free labor abroad began to widen it became apparent that a special committee to consolidate this activity was imperative. Responding to this need, the International Labor Relations Committee was formed in 1950, under the chairmanship of Matthew Woll, with William Green, George Meany, George M. Harrison, David Dubinsky, John P. Frey, A. E. Lyon, William J. McSorley and Lee W. Minton as members, and Florence Thorne as secretary.

Pledging the AFL primarily as a force for world peace, the International Labor Relations Committee has forged ahead with an active program for a democratic foreign policy, for help toward full recovery of democratic Europe, and, above all, for the mobilization of all free labor forces into a positive and constructive alignment to resist and eventually to eliminate the Moscow-ruled World Federation of Trade Unions still masquerading as a trade union world labor center.

Even before World War II, when Nazi and Fascist violence was shaping up as a barbaric manhunt bent on liquidating every leader of labor and exponent of democracy, Labor's League for Human Rights, launched by Matthew Woll, was carrying out a series of nationwide drives to help trade union underground fighters to escape the deadly claws of totalitarian tyranny. During the war years, the League continued its remarkable rescue work in cooperation with other free labor agencies, in addition to supplying funds and food to individuals and groups of labor men and women abroad who kept on fighting courageously against the Black, Brown and Red fiends.

AFL's "Voice" Abroad

Another arm of the AFL's trade union world campaign has been the Free Trade Union Committee, a publishing agency set up on the initiative of Matthew Woll some five years ago. Its monthly publication, "The International Free Trade Union News," has appeared in four languages—English, French, German and Italian. Scores of thousands of this journal have reached regularly trade union activists everywhere, some copies of the "News" being smuggled even into the Kremlin's satellite countries. The "News" actually has become the AFL's "voice" in trade union affairs to the world beyond America's borders. The Free Trade Union Committee has also published a number of pamphlets and booklets dealing in an informative way with current international labor problems.

In discussing, with obvious pride, the far-flung activities of the AFL's "foreign office," President Green has recently observed: "Probably the most important task our Federation has been tackling in this field of international relations is the maintenance on a permanent basis of AFL representatives and bureaus abroad. In addition to our chief international representative, George P. Delaney, we have two special men in Western Europe, and we have one in India. We also have a bureau in Formosa from where we are in touch with the growing resistance movement on the Chinese mainland. We are also about to establish two other bureaus to help free labor in the Far East. Our 'diplomatic corps' has its work cut out for it. Their task is to keep in close touch with labor in their vast areas, to go wherever and whenever duty calls—in Europe, Asia, the Near or the Far East to promote trade union democracy and to cancel out Communist infiltration in labor.

"There's not an important labor convention in the free world where the AFL voice is not heard, through our spokesmen, and these voices are welcome and appreciated. Recently, we have helped to establish in Paris the 'International Free Trade Union Center-in-Exile'

60

and are obtaining many contacts with resistance movements behind the Iron Curtain.

"Entering New Era"

"We have entered a new era in domestic and world affairs, and the direction which the trade union and political labor movements take in the years immediately ahead of us in this battle of ideas will determine in a large measure which way Europe will go in the ensuing struggle between democracy and dictatorship.

"This, however, is not all the work we are doing in the international field, though it may not strictly relate to labor. We have been for a number of years now in the United Nations, in an advisory capacity on one of its most important councils, the UNESCO. We, of the AFL, I may say it with some pride, took the initiative in proposing the draft for a 'Bill of Human Rights' which later became a model for the International Bill of Rights adopted by the United Nations. And it was our consultants who raised the burning issue of slave labor in Russia's 'corrective' camps. We have thus helped to expose the slave nature of a large part of the Soviet economy, a charge that these so-called champions of labor have not been able to refute even in part.

"And when the Communists of France and Italy conspired to sabotage the delivery of American arms to the North Atlantic Pact nations on Moscow's orders, it was the assistance given by the AFL to democratic labor that nipped that Red plot and kept Europe's ports free for the shipments of defense arms.

"And the support which our great membership has given to this program of help to free labor on every continent—whether it be Germany, China, Israel, Finland, India, Italy or Japan—has been undivided and intense. Anyone who has visited our conventions in recent years and watched the deep interest with which our delegates receive the annual reports of the Committee on International Labor Relations can easily convince himself of this.

"And it seems to me in vain to debate, at this day, the relative importance of Asia and Europe to the strategy of opposition to Communism. We cannot afford the luxury of a choice between the two. Both are vital and all the weapons we can muster are needed. The price is high, but no price is too high for the preservation of human liberty and world peace," President Green summed up.

Aiding Jewish Nazi Victims

The Jewish Labor Committee, a group representing trade unions and fraternal labor organizations with close to a half-million members, was formed through the initiative of the late B. Charney Vladeck, famed labor and civic leader, shortly after the Nazis came to power in Germany in 1933. Hitler's first step was to destroy the German labor movement and to imprison or liquidate its leaders. Along with this drive against organized labor, the Nazis launched a genocide campaign against Jews.

The primary aim of the Jewish Labor Committee at the time of its formation was to help the victims of Nazism and Fascism, trade unionists as well as the racial victims of the Nazis, the Jews. In the years that followed the Jewish Labor Committee supported every endeavor to fight Nazism—the underground movement in Germany and the resistance and rescue forces in France under the Nazi occupation. It extended a helping hand to the resistance groups in Poland and occupied Norway. In the postwar years, the Jewish Labor Committee combined a program of rehabilitation of the shattered remnants of the Jewish people in Europe with an energetic campaign of combating bigotry and intolerance at home. In this it has received magnificent support from the trade unions, with AFL President William Green setting the pace.

President Green's interest in the rescue work and the anti-bigotry crusades of the Jewish Labor Committee goes back to 1940 when his direct personal appeal to Secretary of State Cordell Hull resulted in the rescue of some 1,500 European labor leaders from the claws of Hitler and Stalin. The rescued men and women were settled in the free lands of Europe and in the Western Hemisphere. During the terrible years of 1941–43, when Hitler's bloody minions were slaughtering millions of non-combatant Jews and other helpless minorities, William

Green joined the frantic efforts of the Jewish Labor Committee to urge the State Department and the chancelleries in the remaining free lands of Europe to warn the Nazis that they would be held individually responsible for genocidal crimes. Unfortunately, what at that time appeared as exigencies of war strategy and divided counsels among European leaders stood in the way of energetic remonstrations and many more millions perished.

In Anti-Bigotry Drive

In 1946, when the Jewish Labor Committee launched a drive against racial discrimination and religious bigotry on domestic levels, President Green called upon all AFL unions to cooperate in this campaign. In the years that followed every AFL convention adopted resolutions in favor of the anti-bigotry movement. At the San Francisco convention in 1947, the Jewish Labor Committee together with the Negro Labor Committee, the Catholic Interracial Council and the Presbyterian Institute of Industrial Relations, presented a bronze plaque to William Green for "his courageous battle for people's rights in the endless crusade for freedom of conscience and the dignity of man." Charles S. Zimmerman and A. Philip Randolph made the presentation.

William Green's concern with economic opportunity for workers of all racial or national strains has mounted with the years. He kept hammering at the individual state federations for support of national and state fair employment practices commissions. On April 30, 1949, he appeared as principal speaker at a civil rights conference sponsored by the Chicago Federation of Labor which was attended by some 700 delegates from all AFL locals in that city. "From its very inception," President Green told the Chicago unionists, "the AFL pledged itself to combat racial and religious prejudice and man's inhumanity to man. . . . In a broad sense, intolerance must be eradicated in America as a measure of national safety and in defense of our free democratic institutions. Who are those on the other side of this fight? Who are those who are making capital out of intolerance? Who are those who resist so bitterly the extension of civil rights to all American citizens? They are the same filibusterers, the same reactionaries and the same die-hard obstructionists who have teamed up immemorially against the underprivileged, against organized labor and against all economic, social and political progress."

"His Brother's Keeper"

Culminating tribute to William Green for a decade of unceasing work in behalf of millions of human beings battered by storms of hate, reaction and persecution was paid him at a testimonial "Assembly" at the Waldorf-Astoria in New York City on the afternoon of October 28, 1951, under the auspices of the Jewish Labor Committee at which more than 2,000 labor and community leaders watched the unveiling of a bronze bust of the AFL's president. George Meany, Secretary-Treasurer of the AFL, spoke of William Green as "one who has done more than any other living American to promote the humanitarian causes of the Jewish Labor Committee and has given service 'far beyond the call of duty' to rescue the oppressed and the persecuted."

Sharing with Meany the speakers' platform were U. S. Vice President Alben W. Barkley, Secretary of Labor Maurice J. Tobin, and David Dubinsky, president of the ILGWU. In responding to the high tribute paid him, President Green, with characteristic humility, remarked: "No service has ever afforded me greater satisfaction than this work which I, together with my friends of the Jewish Labor Committee, have engaged in in the past. . . . It might perhaps be easier and less taxing for American trade unionists to wash their hands of the misfortunes of those in other lands and to say, as some other groups in the community appear to be saying—'Am I my brother's keeper?' But to do so would be to break faith with those basic principles which lie at the very foundation of the trade union movement, which tell us that we are indeed our brother's keeper and that so long as our brothers are in chains, we are bound with them. Our own freedom will never be safe as long as others are enslaved."

Firm on Fascism

When William Green assumed the presidency of the AFL in the end of 1924, Italy was already fast in the grip of Fascism with Benito Mussolini riding roughshod with his Blackshirts over the vanishing liberties of the Italian people. In the United States, however, workers of Italian descent were proceeding to join by the thousand labor unions —in the construction trades, in the garment industry, in textiles and various other occupations—and reaping the benefits of free, organized labor.

Some two years before, Green had made his first contact with organized Italian workers in this country when as secretary-treasurer of the United Mine Workers, he addressed the young Italian Dressmakers Union, Local 89, ILGWU, seeking support for his miners engaged at that time in a prolonged and bitter strike. The Italian dressmakers responded warmly to his appeal.

A rugged opponent of autocracy in any hue or form, William Green took a firm stand against Fascism from its very inception sharply condemning Mussolini's regime in a widely quoted public statement in which he compared the "menacing influences and sordid infiltrationist practices sponsored in our country by Red Russia and Black Italy." He castigated Mussolini for his complicity in the murder of the brilliant leader of social democracy in the Italian parliament, Giacomo Matteoti, by a Fascist gang in June 1924.

And when in September 1924, groups of democrats, liberals and laborites of Italian descent formed an "Anti-Fascist Alliance," Green addressed its first assembly and prophetically declared: "I am certain that the Italian workers now deprived of their freedom will continue to fight until they will regain what they have lost." In the name of the Federation, he pledged that its membership "will always be at your side to help chase Fascism away from the face of the earth."

That same year, when the AFL met in convention in Detroit, Green told the delegates how deeply he had been impressed by the sincerity and "fighting quality" of the Anti-Fascist Alliance's congress and

65

the convention approved a strong resolution against Fascism and the Mussolini rule in Italy. From then on, the Italian anti-Fascist elements felt confident that they had the full weight of America's labor movement on their side.

All-Out Aid for Italy's Labor

President Green's support and the Federation's friendship for the anti-Fascist cause spiraled after Mussolini, at Hitler's behest, declared war on America a few days after Pearl Harbor. The Italian-American Labor Council, a body composed exclusively of trade unions with Italian-speaking memberships and presided over by Luigi Antonini, ILGWU first vice president, came into being both as a challenge to Mussolini's arrogance and as the true voice of organized Italian labor in this country. One of the Council's first acts, which at once received the full support of President Green and of the AFL, was a move to exempt Italian non-citizens residing here from the enemy alien category in which they found themselves as a consequence of Mussolini's war. This move proved successful when Attorney General Francis Biddle granted the Council's request on Columbus Day 1942. This action scored a significant victory against Fascism in this country.

Green did not stop at this point in aiding Italian labor-democratic forces to destroy the Fascist regime. During the war he joined in a number of short-wave broadcasts to Italian workers across the ocean urging civil disobedience against the Fascist dictator. In the spring of 1943, when the Mussolini regime fell apart and Italy's unconditional surrender was announced, William Green in a public statement declared, "Italy's surrender marks the beginning of the collapse of the Axis. . . . The Italian people have not lost, they have gained, they have won freedom from the yoke of Fascism and the opportunity to govern themselves in the future as a free and democratic country." Shortly thereafter, the AFL president designated Luigi Antonini as the Federation's representative on a joint delegation with the British Trades Union Congress to go to Italy after the liberation of Rome and help in the rebuilding of an Italian free trade union movement.

A Just Peace to New Italy

In the years that followed, William Green has supported the Italian-American Labor Council in all efforts to assure adequate American relief to liberated Italy; to have Italy recognized as a co-belligerent, and to press for a just peace for a new Italy. When in 1946 Luigi Antonini went to the Paris Peace Conference to seek in the name of the Italian-American Labor Council a just peace for Italy, William Green authorized him to speak also on behalf of the AFL. Italy's admission to the United Nations, which has been strongly favored by the AFL since the United Nations was formed in 1945, has been consistently thwarted by Soviet vetoes in the Security Council. During the hotly contested Italian elections in the spring of 1948, William Green made several appeals to the Italian voters in behalf of democracy which were radioed in Italian across the Atlantic.

Green was given the "Four Freedoms" award by the Italian-American Labor Council at its tenth anniversary fete in December 1951. Previous recipients of this award were the late President Franklin D. Roosevelt, former Attorney General Francis Biddle, and General Mark W. Clark. The award to President Green read in part: "In appreciation and recognition of his fearless and unceasing struggle against national and racial discrimination, poverty, dictatorship and war . . . and magnificent services in enabling American democracy to meet its new responsibilities of world leadership in the fight for freedom and peace."

Champions Israeli Labor

On January 11, 1951, 1,500 men and women prominent in the world of labor and leaders in the Greater New York Jewish community assembled to do honor to William Green in recognition of his lifelong interest in the Histadrut—the Israeli Labor Federation—and his unbroken concern with the destiny and independence of the young Jewish State of Israel still surrounded by a ring of mortal enemies. The meeting was arranged by the American Trade Union Council in support of the Histadrut.

In responding to the many speeches which hailed his champion-
ship of Jewish organized labor in Israel, William Green drew a
parallel between "the aims and ideals of the AFL and those who gave
their strength, energy and even their lives that Israel may live as more
than a dream" and found them identical. "Histadrut," he declared,
"has been the mainstay of the entire society of Israel." He pointed to
the economic and social attainments of the Histadrut—the 8-hour day,
employment through its own labor exchanges, seniority, family allow-
ances, sick leave and vacations with pay, and social insurance. Histadrut, he said, has developed its own system of schools to improve the
level of education. In a country with little investment capital, Histadrut has established cooperative industries to help maintain a high rate
of employment. Most important of all, President Green said, was the
illuminating fact that all of this has been achieved without yielding to
temptations to abandon the principles of liberty, democracy and
equality and resort to authoritarian methods—even in the face of crisis
and hunger.

35 Years of Friendship

The following paragraphs are from the pen of Harry Lang, a veteran journalist who knew well Samuel Gompers and has been for many
years a friend of William Green:

"In 1917 Green was a member of the sub-committee of the
AFL's Executive Council to consider the report of the American
Alliance for Labor and Democracy on President Wilson's foreign
policy. In this report there was mention of the Balfour Declaration
for a Jewish national home in Palestine. He heard the views of the
State Department. The sub-committee recommended the approval
of the Balfour Declaration, underscoring 'the legitimate rights of
the Jewish people to a homeland in Palestine,' and urged the
United States to advocate this at the peace conferences. The Executive Council approved the report and the AFL convention ratified it.

"Early in 1919, Green went with the American labor delegation to Europe to attempt to set up a trade union international.

68

Upon his return to the United States, Green fought the isolationist anti-Wilson forces and helped to strengthen the international outlook of the AFL.

"In 1928, President Green sent a memorandum to President Coolidge with a resolution adopted at the AFL convention endorsing the Jewish labor movement in Palestine, Histadrut. In 1930 he sent a message to a great protest demonstration in New York against the Passfield White Paper which virtually annulled the Balfour Declaration.

"The upheavals of the 1930s came along. President Green became a tireless anti-Nazi fighter. He fought against the diplomatic recognition of the Soviet regime. He did succeed in convincing Roosevelt to join the International Labor Office, and he helped lead the AFL back into the International Federation of Trade Unions—on the AFL's own terms.

"William Green welcomed the British plan to partition Palestine into Jewish and Arab states, and to demonstrate his warmest sympathy with Jewish aspirations he became a co-sponsor of the Jewish settlement in Galilee named in honor of the great French socialist statesman Leon Blum.

"The Second World War came, and soon William Green became the 'ambassador' of peoples in exile, of wandering labor people, of uprooted social democrats persecuted by Nazis or Communists and often by both diabolical partners. Green took a leading part in opening Stalin's international scandal, the criminal execution of the two Jewish labor leaders of Poland, Henryk Erlich and Victor Alter. And there came to him the underground of the Haganah, who rescued Jews from the shambles of Europe and brought them to Palestine through Italy and France.

"In the days of illegal immigration into Palestine, William Green did not rest. His special affection for the labor movement in the State of Israel has been expressed on innumerable occasions. During the United Nations debate on the future of Palestine, he voiced the support of Jewish claims for nationhood as a free and equal member of the family of nations."

These flash-like, penetrating observations by Harry Lang cast a vivid light on the international labor background of William Green who has managed to give so much of himself to the fierce and demanding causes which have crowded the world arena over the past thirty-five years.

The wonder of it is that he really had been able to do it, and do it so well. For, as George Meany described it on a recent occasion: "Let me point out that Bill Green has a full-time job as president of the AFL. When I say 'full time' I am understating the facts. Business matters and conferences have a way of overtaking him even at breakfast, luncheon and dinner—and after dinner as well. Yet, he has always found time to do the many extra jobs which his mind and heart commanded him to do."

Aid to "City of Hope"

Organized labor's accelerated interest in community affairs in the past dozen years, a tendency which has won practically unanimous support from every international union affiliated with the AFL, got its strongest spurt during the war years when the emotional surge radiating from the global struggle and repeated calls for relief for various causes "till it hurt" swept the land.

William Green took the lead in responding to these patriotic and humanitarian wartime appeals. But above and beyond the war needs affecting fighting men and returning veterans, President Green saw also the need of combating the illnesses which daily affect wage-earners and low-income people in particular, his own folks, so to say. He watched the inroads which tuberculosis and, of late years, cancer had been making among workpeople who cannot afford the prohibitive costs of hospitalization and he promptly enlisted in behalf of organized help to these victims.

His pet philanthropy shortly became the "City of Hope," a great medical center located in the hills outside Los Angeles, started in 1912 as a tuberculosis sanatorium, chiefly for trade unionists and their families. Green was attracted to the "City of Hope" because it practiced what its motto, phrased in the words of the immortal Louis Pasteur, preached: "We do not ask of an unfortunate, what country do you

70

come from or what is your religion? We say to him: you suffer, that's enough. You belong to us; we shall make you well."

Beginning with the ILGWU in 1920, which donated money for the construction of a wing and of a library, union wings were endowed at the "City of Hope" by the Bakery and Confectionery Workers, the Hatters and Millinery International Union and, currently, the Amalgamated Meat Cutters and the Hotel and Restaurant Employees' Union are putting up special buildings at the "City of Hope" for their members. For the past five years, the "City of Hope" has had cooperating with it a National Labor Council of which William Green is honorary chairman.

For a Gompers Wing

Over the past three decades, AFL unions alone have contributed more than $1,000,000 to the "City of Hope." On organized labor's initiative, combined labor-management support has also been encouraged for this unique hospital which depends entirely upon voluntary contributions. In the last few years, several major AFL unions, including the Teamsters and the Machinists, have been showing interest in long-term hospitalization needs for tubercular patients at the "City of Hope."

William Green paid a special visit last year, after the close of the 1951 AFL convention in San Francisco, to the great medical center in Los Angeles. Upon his return to Washington, he enlisted the help of the Executive Council and of Secretary-Treasurer George Meany for the erection of a Samuel Gompers memorial wing at the "City of Hope." In May, 1952, the "City of Hope's" National Labor Council tendered a testimonial dinner to George Meany in "evidence of his awareness of the role this hospital is playing as a medical fraternal ally in labor's efforts to demand equal facilities for the sick, despite financial inability to pay."

Salvaging Ex-TB Victims

One other non-sectarian institution serving the needs of men and women of low-income groups, largely wage-earners who had been stricken with tuberculosis and were being re-trained after cure in various skills for self-subsistence, attracted the attention of top AFL officers, including President William Green, Secretary-Treasurer George Meany and Vice President Matthew Woll.

It is the Ex-Patients' Tubercular Home of Denver, Colo., catering to the needs of discharged TB patients from Colorado sanatoria and seeking for them occupational outlets and adjustments for normal living. In most instances, these ex-patients leave the hospitals still badly in need of complete recuperation and without visible means of support. The Denver Ex-Patients' Home has engaged in this rehabilitation work with exceptional success for the past 44 years.

It was only natural that the Denver Ex-Patients' Home, most of whose inmates are workers, should turn for help to organized labor and fraternal labor societies. Ten years ago, an advisory committee consisting of leading trade unionists was formed to accelerate moral and financial support for this TB rehabilitation center. President Green, in urging support for the Denver Ex-Patients' Home, stressed the point that it was catering to all TB victims on the way to recovery, regardless of creed or nationality, and offering them free food, shelter, medical treatment and the kindest care and guidance for an unlimited period of time.

Portrait—and Parallel

Any attempt to assess the stature of William Green on the broad canvas of American labor history invariably conjures up a comparison with his predecessor, Samuel Gompers, if only for the mere reason that since its formation, back in 1881, the AFL really has had but two presidents.

Paralleling the two Federation presidents on the basis of historic sum-ups or concrete balances is not an easy matter. Both Samuel Gompers and William Green had similar humble beginnings—both were born and raised in environments of hard toil, which sent them in their early teens to work for a pittance—Sam Gompers as a tobacco stripper and, later, as a cigarmaker, and young Bill Green as a water boy for a railroad gang and, at sixteen, as a helper to his father in a soft coal mine. Both of them physically rugged and with but a smattering of schooling, they had early in their youth become avid readers during their few leisure hours.

The slums of London and of New York's East Side and the glum, grimy small Ohio coal town were two worlds apart in last century's midway years, but the struggles and yearnings of the folks who lived there and called it "home" differed little. And the fierce, relentless faith in the possibility of winning for his fellow workingmen a little more security and a little better life which drove on young Sam Gompers to fight for a cigarmakers' union and later led him across many battles to found the modern American labor movement, has served also as the mainspring for William Green's utter dedication to unionism and sharpened his gifts for leadership as the ideal successor to Samuel Gompers.

A Grand Welfare Program

Doubtless, there are many and substantial differences between William Green and Samuel Gompers, personality distinctions which invoke a variety of specific spiritual and mental endowments, though both stand four-square on the fundamentals of labor economics as the cornerstone of trade unionism. Still, while Gompers visualized social and political implementation as a mere accessory in the struggle for the improvement of labor's well-being—an accessory often to be treated with suspicion as a factor likely to impair the potency and freedom of trade unions, William Green, though a staunch trade unionist first and last, has ranged far beyond the economic milieu in search for endowing the labor movement with greater voltage. William Green has not hesitated to reach out of the wage-hour limits to set a fast pace in the fight for raising standards of living for America's wage-earners through labor legislation. To William Green social security laws, wage-hour enactments, elimination of racial and religious discrimination in job-getting as well as in other civil opportunities through state and national legislation have become part of labor's daily chores.

"Co-Existence" Is "Voluntarism"

His critics, many of them rank detractors—and they have ranged all the way from the extreme right in politics and industry to the extreme left, with a sprinkling of the "intelligentsia" forever sighing for the emergence of a "strong" man on the labor arena among them—have time and again tried to paint William Green as a docile executive who has left no marked imprint on the labor history or policies of his time. That this is willful myopia need hardly be emphasized. It is true, of course, that William Green, like Samuel Gompers before him, has never paraded up and down the national scene as a labor "czar," nor has he ever attempted to override the will of his associates when he found himself in a minority. "Voluntarism," the principle of organizational co-existence which Samuel Gompers had laid down as his own credo and to which he adhered as chief executive of the union he founded, has remained the basic principle of union government in the AFL in relation to his fellow associates on the Executive Council throughout William Green's presidency.

The striking fact remains that William Green has been chosen to lead the Federation for 28 years without a contest, without even serious opposition, despite the fact that he actually has had no major union claiming him as its "favorite son." When first selected by the Executive Council to fill the interim period as president shortly after Gompers died after the 1924 convention, the newspapers gave wide currency to rumors that Green's elevation was but a temporary shift arranged by John L. Lewis, so that he might take it away later. This canard soon vanished as year after year, even after the United Mine Workers had been pulled out of the AFL, the Coshocton miner continued to be re-elected to the presidency.

"For the Littlest as for the Biggest"

Having no special axes to grind and not personally disposed to reach out for extra-curricular power, William Green continued to enhance his prestige with the years as a leader who is as considerate of the fair claims of the small unions as of the big ones. "My business is to protect, as far as my means and ability permit me, the legitimate interests of all the unions in the Federation, the littlest of them no less than the biggest," he has continually asserted.

Cool, level-headed, conservative, yet aggressive when aroused to fighting pitch, William Green, fully conscious that as president of the Federation he is no solo performer, always has acted as chairman of an executive group representing autonomous bodies of organized workers, each of them a self-governing "sovereignty," and each very jealous of its autonomy. Yet, in close association with these vigorously independent men, who would bow to no dictator, President William Green has managed to keep the Federation upon a course which in all its broad lines followed consistently his own humanistic concepts. American trade unionism, it has been repeatedly proven, not only will not stomach a home-grown dictator of any hue but actually believes that it can get along best without one.

What the outside world thinks of William Green, veteran oracle of eight million American wage-earners, was compactly expressed in a few discerning words sent by U. S. Supreme Court Justice William O. Douglas last year to a New York gathering of labor men and civic leaders who came to honor the AFL president. Said the eminent Supreme Court liberal:

> "William Green has been in the forefront of dozens of campaigns for social justice and human welfare. He has made articulate the aspirations of millions who cannot speak for themselves. He has furnished leadership which has been courageous. His work at home and abroad has won for him the gratitude of peoples of many races and tongues."

THE UNION AND THE FUTURE OF DEMOCRACY

By William Green

*(Below are reproduced the essential parts of a chapter from William Green's book, "**LABOR AND DEMOCRACY**," which appeared in 1939 and was published by the Princeton University Press. Today this book is a collector's item and can be found only in a few of the largest public and university libraries. We reprint it, with grateful acknowledgment to the publishers, because it basically presents President Green's credo with regard to American trade unionism and its inseverability from the mainstreams of the country's life and its impacts on the future of democratic society, at home and abroad. Though written some 13 years ago, on the very eve of World War II, when, in the words of William Green, "great fear again clutched the world," its diagnoses, conclusions and "commandments" sound as timely and as relevant today as in 1939. Like then, fear of expanding totalitarian aggression—Red imperialism instead of Brown barbarism—grips the world and shapes its thought and action.—Editor)*

AGAIN a great fear clutches the world. What we had hailed in two great countries of Europe as revolutions for democracy have turned into revolutions destructive of our old civilizations. Two countries in the grip of power politics have overthrown the old order within their own territory. They have repudiated old standards of ethics, overthrown religion, and wrecked a social order that had evolved through centuries of ideals and through countless struggles to realize them. Freedom is no longer the ideal of the state or the ideal of revolution; power, compulsion, regimentation are the new political and social procedures. The citizens and the resources of a nation are mobilized in accord with plans for national aggrandizement, terror, persecution, and perversion of technical progress to purposes of destruction that foreshadow the decline and demoralization of the nations.

Democracies, with their belief in private property and freedom for the individual, have founded a social order on principles of integrity and mutual good faith that rest upon respect for ethical standards. Democracies have sought progress through assuring constantly broadening groups the right to returns on the product of their labor. Our relations with our fellow men rest upon observance of accepted standards of behavior. The moment principles are renounced there is no guide for human relations. The chaos of savagery displaces civilization. Now these revolutions have overrun national barriers. The answer of democracy must represent coordinated policy and authority.

THE FUTURE of democracy on all continents as well as here in the United States lies largely in the hands of labor. Wage earners and their families constitute the great majority of the people. It is primarily the workers and the other under-privileged who gain new opportunity with each forward step in establishing for every human being real opportunity for his progress in all the relationships of our common life.

Wage earners are helpless without the opportunity for progress which democracy provides. We want to see an end of starvation on this earth—whether starvation for food or for the opportunity of living a good life. This is our special interest. Democracy is not confined to the political or economic fields; it is a way of living applied to the whole of existence. It implies principles of freedom that must continuously be applied to human relationships under changing conditions. Democracy does not bring the dead-levels of regimentation, but experience with democratic procedures develops discrimination and the realization that identical provisions for all do not necessarily result in equal opportunity for all. Democracy assures individual freedom. To work out the transition from a social structure that provides special privilege for those in position of power, to a social order providing equal opportunity for all, is something that challenges both our intelligence and our integrity of purpose.

The totalitarian state denies the competence of democracy either to maintain efficient government or to plan and control its industries for the best service of society. Political chaos resulting from power politics and the struggle for domain together with world-wide depression gave opportunity to set up dictatorships in Europe with absolute political and economic control. Unrestricted power facilitates action.

DEMOCRACIES, because applying the principles of representation and consent of the governed, move slowly in crises, but they have the strength inherent of cooperation in applying decisions reached by democratic channels. In the long run voluntary cooperation outlives the rule of force. Representation and majority rule are inseparable from democracy. Countries reluctant to work out their destinies have turned to dictators as an escape from the obligations of democracy. Instead of finding peaceful solutions for the political and economic problems of their countries, dictators relied on force and built up huge military reserves. As was inevitable, again within the span of twenty-five years Europe is plunged into the horrors of modern warfare and the peace of the world is threatened. The progress toward world democracy that we hoped for through the Versailles Treaty, which ended a war fought for democracy, was blocked by mistakes of the Treaty and the failure of the League of Nations to function in the spirit of democracy. It was hampered by the failure of some of the democracies to participate.

As labor in the United States again faces international problems and situations similar to those of the World War, we realize that democracy cannot be gained on the battlefield. Democracy gains opportunity only through agreements for cooperation established at conference tables, and achieves reality in proportion as democratic principles control our thoughts and actions. Labor in the United States is not a sect or a class but a cross-section of our nation, sharing in national ideals but with a special passion for democracy born of our struggle to extend its application within our daily living. Absence of democratic opportunity has meant to us absence of economic security, denial of civil liberties, denial of safeguards for body and health in the workshops, meager provisions for our families and dependents.

WHETHER in peace or in war, the major obligation we have as a people is to maintain principles of democracy within our own boundaries in order that justice may result from all of our dealings and that all may have that freedom of living that is essential to personal dignity. We scarcely realize the possibilities of democracy, and in practice we still deny to many equal opportunity for progress. But our vision of what democracy offers to human beings is what binds us to our government and makes us proud to be citizens. It is this vision that makes ours a land of opportunity. Without it we would be poor in spirit.

Since the principles of democracy are our most precious heritage, established through a war for freedom and maintained even at the expense of civil warfare, it is our stern obligation to see to it that they are not lost during our stewardship. The essential principles are few and clear-cut:

First. The right of representation in order to have a voice in the determination of decisions affecting our welfare. The right of representation relates not only to the political field but wherever welfare is concerned. For labor, it refers first of all to the work relationship. The right of representation is barren unless it rests on free choice. In totalitarian countries the first move for dictatorship is suppression of free unions. Forewarned that this is the key to maintenance of democracy in the United States, it is my responsibility and the responsibility of all organized labor to keep our unions free, devoted to the ideals and practices of democracy within the union and in outside relations, truly representative of the needs and ideals of those who work for wages and dedicated to the welfare of wage earners as citizens of a democracy.

Second. Employer-employee or work relations should be defined in a work contract stipulating terms and conditions of work and machinery for adjusting differences arising under the contract. Such contracts must be negotiated by representatives of the parties concerned. This principle should be applied whether employment is in private or public industry—or whether industry is under a peace or war economy.

Third. The functional elements in an industry are finance, management, production and sales to consumers. When functional agencies

80

or boards are constituted for control purposes, such as the War Resources Board, all of these functional elements should have representation on that agency. Labor, which constitutes the operating staff of an industry, is also the most important resource of the nation and is entitled to representation under both considerations. It is self-evident that whenever a democratic government sets up an agency to deal with a problem, the welfare of its citizens is its primary concern. Labor, or those citizens directly concerned with operating an industry, should always have adequate representation on all governmental control or policy-making agencies.

Fourth. The strength of a nation, whether for constructive work or national defense, lies in the sureness with which it accords justice to all its people. The discrimination with which a democracy assures economic and personal justice within its own territory, is the measure of the power of the nation under emergencies. Whether for peace or war, we strengthen a nation when we remedy the causes of social and economic unrest.

Fifth. Democracy must not use the controls of dictators to mould public opinion and action. Decisions upon education should be made locally, and control over dissemination of information should be in the hands of voluntary organizations. Society should insist upon fair play, honesty and respect for facts.

THE AMERICAN Federation of Labor has earned the right to its acceptance as a tried American institution. Essentially democratic in spirit and in procedure, we have learned to look upon our interests and welfare as related to the interests and welfare of all others concerned in the same problems, and have sought progress through coordinated programs.

Over a period of six decades we have established principles of action and procedures that have established their usefulness by constructive results. Through union organization and collective bargaining, we created the agencies for justice and progress in the economic field, thus laying a foundation for a democratic way of life in this and related fields. Through legislation and political action we have functioned as citizens of a democracy, utilizing the constitutional methods available to promote our welfare. We have sought opportunity to participate with other citizens, not over any individuals or groups. Through legislation we have attempted to gain opportunity for progress and basic standards of social security. Under all circumstances we have sought to keep open opportunity for change and progress and have opposed regimentation and arbitrary control. We have regarded ourselves as a part of a nation and have tried to coordinate our welfare with the whole of social progress.

In the World War we served in the military forces and in the industries necessary for military and civilian life. While we tried to assure democracy to those for whom we were primarily responsible, we integrated our activity with purposes of national welfare. To our wartime policies is due a considerable measure of credit for maintaining democratic procedure even under war administration.

IN PEAK peacetime industrial prosperity, though harassed with un-American plans to displace free trade unions, the American Federation of Labor developed the procedures of union-management cooperation and proposed a partnership for labor in industries based upon the investment of their labor, skill and creative ability. Union-management cooperation enables labor to contribute more to management because mutuality of interests is accepted as the basis for cooperation. We made our contribution to efforts to set up industrial order through voluntary organization.

In the world depression that shattered the foundations of our industrial structure, we maintained our union organization and cooperated with the government to work out social control of industry through legislation. Our insistence upon equal opportunity for labor has been a bulwark against Fascist or Communist tendencies. With the right to membership in unions of our choice assured by the government, we hope progressively to realize the rich possibilities of a democratic way of living. Our own organizations are only chains of human hands, held together by common needs and objectives and dependent upon the integrity of the common cause for continued power and influence.

The American labor movement, with all its shortcomings and imperfections, is the keystone of democracy in our national life. I am proud to be in its service.

"WE AND THE WORLD"

(Ten years later, speaking at the concluding session of the founding Congress of the International Confederation of Free Trade Unions in London, England, on Dec. 8, 1949, Pres. William Green had another occasion to state before a great assembly of free trade unionists from 53 countries representing nearly 50 million workers, in a concise and clear-cut form, some sharply revealing facts and observations bearing on American organized labor's expanding interest in free trade unionism the world over as a part of democracy's global effort to combat totalitarian tyranny and dictatorship.—Editor)

It is slanderous to say that America has become rich as a result of the war. What we have attained has been gotten *not* through occupying or expropriating little or big countries or taking even one cent of reparations or one foot of soil from defeated countries. We have progressed solely by dint of hard, efficient, free labor in a free country blessed with great natural resources. In fact, in the last war, the American people paid a very high price in life and limb, in human casualties for our common victory. We also paid a colossal material price. We have used up in behalf of our common victory over $400 billion worth of our national and natural wealth.

We are determined to help win the peace for democracy, human welfare and dignity, just as decisively as we helped in winning the war. Through the Marshall Plan and other projects, our country has spent well over $60 billion in various undertakings to rescue from famine men, women and children in every part of the world, and in helping those nations—former foe and friend alike—that are free to help themselves in reconstructing their economies.

85

The average American has been contributing through taxes about $150 a year towards payment of this bill. We do not ask for thanks or crave gratitude. We do not propose to dictate the politics or economic forms of any recipient nation. We work and give and will give again and again because we realize that our privileged world position and our unswerving loyalty to the ideals of human freedom, decency and peace put new responsibilities upon us.

. . . The American economy is anything but perfect. We must overcome the lingering evils of racialism. But we do have the right and the possibility to change and readjust. American labor has an increasing right and mounting might to assure that these changes are for the better —for the economic and social well-being of the people. That and that alone is what makes our economy free.

Different countries have different historical backgrounds and different stages and trends of economic development. We are not trying to impose our economic forms on any nation. But we are just as firmly opposed to anyone imposing economic forms on us.

In an economic sense, the world is being integrated. No one country can long stay prosperous in an impoverished world. . . . By the same token, no prosperity can long continue in a world terrified and paralyzed by the fear of war. We love and want peace. We seek and demand and work for international peace and security. Labor has been the traditional champion of and fighter for the realization of this lofty objective. But we must never forget one very important fact. Though it takes two to make and keep the peace, it takes only one to break the peace and plunge mankind into a conflagration.

The basic ideals and interests of labor are the same throughout the world. However, in different countries, for various reasons, different tactics are employed by free labor to further and achieve these common ends.

The free trade unions of the world now face a world-wide totalitarian conspiracy. This conspiracy has aimed to foist on the workers of all free countries a system of economic exploitation and political oppression which would set labor back hundreds of years. It would rob workers of their human political and social rights. It would degrade their position as individual human beings. It would convert the free trade unions into company unions with the state as the sole employer. It would pervert our unions into mere auxiliaries and departments of the totalitarian Communist parties with monopoly control of all political life.

. . . There is no conflict between living idealism and political progressive action. The high standards and conditions secured by American labor prove this . . . I can see nothing more practical in the program of our new world organization than a frontal, aggressive fight against the enemies of world reconstruction, against all foes of human freedom, against all those who seek world domination through aggression, against all the opponents of orderly, peaceful progress. In this same spirit I can see nothing more idealistic than to assure, through practical everyday trade union action, the constant improvement of the working and living conditions of the laboring people of every nation, regardless of race, color or creed. . . . This is living international labor solidarity.

THROUGH THE CAMERA'S "EYE"

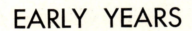

EARLY YEARS

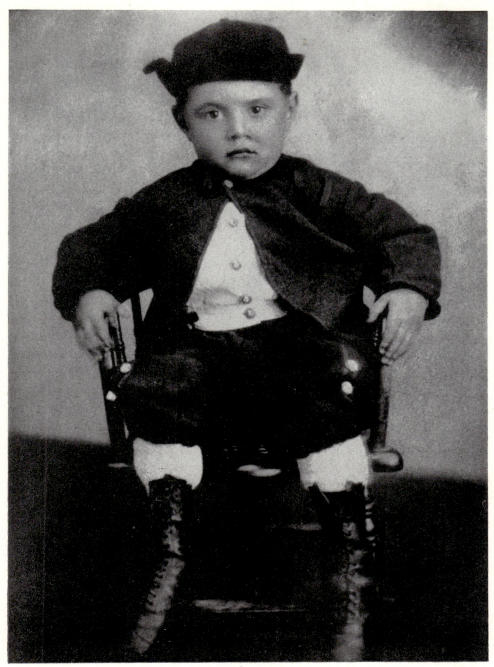

"Billy" Green at 4.

When You Vote, Mark Your Ballot Thus:

| X | FOR STATE SENATOR
WM. GREEN |

(Second Term)

18th-19th District   Democratic Ticket

At turn of century.

Senate-minded miner.

A candidate in quest of votes.

A rising young citizen of Coshocton, Ohio.

UMW SECRETARY—AFL PRESIDENT

American Federation of Labor delegation to the Paris Peace Conference, January-April, 1919. Seated (l. to r.): first vice-president James Duncan, President Samuel Gompers. Standing (l. to r.): third vice-president Frank Duffy, fourth vice-president William Green, former third vice-president John R. Alpine.

It was 1925, the first year of William Green's presidency. Members of the Executive Council (l. to r.) (standing): Thomas A. Rickert, Matthew Woll, Jacob Fischer. Seated (l. to r.): Frank Duffy, Secretary Frank Morrison, William Green.

In darkest year, 20 years ago—The Executive Council of the AFL shown leaving the White House after presenting to President Hoover a plea to support Senator Costigan's bill for direct relief to millions of jobless. Front row, (l. to r.) are: Matthew Woll; Joe N. Weber; J. A. Wilson; Frank Morrison, AFL Secretary; William Green, AFL President; Frank Duffy; John Coefield; T. A. Rickert. Back row, G. M. Bugniazet; A. O. Wharton; Martin F. Ryan. The plea brought no results.

Back in 1934, the early NRA days, labor and government teamwork proved effective in hurdling many obstacles. Shown above are (l. to r.): Edward F. McGrady, Assistant Secretary of Labor; AFL President William Green; General Hugh S. Johnson, NRA administrator, and William Collins, AFL general organizer.

On Labor Day, 1934, Fiorello LaGuardia (seated left), Mayor of New York, was principal speaker at a labor celebration at the "Century of Progress Exposition" at World's Fair. A special committee from the AFL, consisting of President William Green (seated right), John Fitzpatrick, president of the Chicago AFL (standing left), and Victor A. Olander, president of Illinois state AFL, came to invite the New York Mayor to address the great gathering.

Textile workers reaffiliate. In a ceremony on May 10, 1939, before the statue of Samuel Gompers on Massachusetts Avenue in Washington, D.C., President William Green returned AFL charter to the United Textile Workers Union. L. to r. are: Frank Morrison, AFL Secretary; Francis Gorman, United Textile Workers president, and William Green.

So desirable yet still so far—Seen above arguing quietly over potentials of "labor peace" are President Green, AFL Vice President Daniel J. Tobin, and Allan S. Heywood, Organizational Director of the CIO, at a recent meeting.

President Green, accompanied by Charles J. MacGowan, president of the International Brotherhood of Boilermakers, and James A. Brownlow, secretary-treasurer of the AFL Metal Trades Department, seen emerging from White House after consultation with President Truman on legislation aimed at rebuilding the American merchant marine.

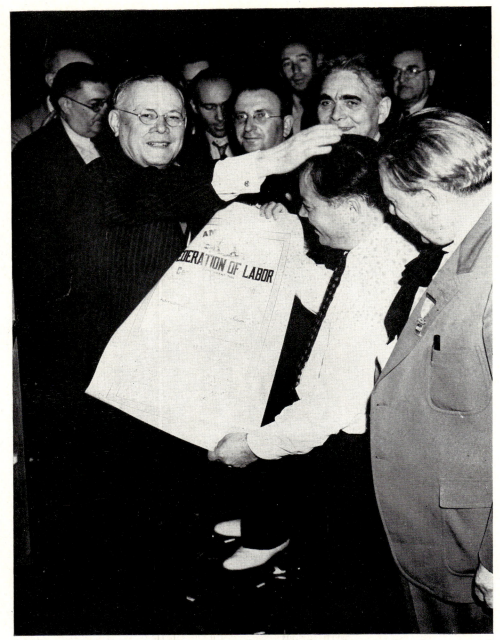

A "day in June" Pres. William Green is not likely to forget, when he returned 40-year-old international charter to the Ladies' Garment Workers at that union's convention early in June, 1940, held in New York's famous Carnegie Hall.

Original oil painting, bearing the legend "AFL 100% FOR DEFENSE," was presented to FDR at White House by Pres. William Green and George Meany, AFL secretary-treasurer, May 26, 1941.

Top—Pres. Green beams on Secretary of Labor Frances Perkins as she steps up to the platform of the 1943 AFL convention held in Boston, Mass.

Bottom—Shown with Pres. William Green is New York's former Lieutenant-Governor Charles Poletti, shortly after he was designated by the Allies as military governor, first of Sicily and Naples, and later of all of North Italy after Mussolini fell in April 1943 and the Italian capital was subsequently liberated.

Pres. Green is shown smiling happily, with Pat Gergen, Fiestabahia queen (at his left) and her maids of honor, at the San Diego Labor Day Jubilee, 1949.

Chairman J. M. Arvey of the Cook County Democratic Committee (left) welcomes Pres. William Green to Chicago where the Executive Council met in October, 1950. Reuben G. Soderstrom, president of Illinois State Federation of Labor, in center.

At 72nd annual convention of the New Jersey State Federation of Labor in Atlantic City, October, 1950, where Pres. Green headed the list of speakers. L. to r.: Vincent J. Murphy, New Jersey Federation's secretary-treasurer; former Under-Secretary of the Army, Archibald S. Alexander, Louis P. Marciante, N. J. federation president, and William Green.

A dramatic moment occurred on March 1, 1951, when all organized labor, acting through the then existing United Labor Policy Committee, voted to pull its representatives out of all defense mobilization agencies. L. to r. are: James B. Carey, CIO secretary-treasurer; AFL President William Green; Elmer Walker, secretary-treasurer, International Association of Machinists, and Art Lyons, secretary Railway Labor Executive Associates.

Assistant Secretary of Defense Anna Rosenberg seen with group of top labor representatives as subject of labor participation on terms of equality in defense matters reached high point in 1951. Flanking her (right) is AFL President William Green with CIO President Philip Murray on her left.

The late wartime War Secretary Robert P. Patterson in a friendly exchange with Pres. Green.

William Lee, Chicago Federation of Labor president, in confab with Pres. William Green at an AFL convention.

IN THE GREATER COMMUNITY

This huge birthday cake, gift of the Bakery and Confectionery Workers' International Union, was presented to President Franklin D. Roosevelt on January 25, 1940. The President and AFL President William Green have a happy time around the cake in the White House. Around the base of each of the 58 candles is a facsimile of a check for $100, presented to the National Infantile Paralysis Foundation by various local labor unions.

Eleanor Roosevelt and Secretary of Labor Frances Perkins pose with AFL President William Green at one of the gala occasions of the New Deal period.

Top—"Voice of Labor" on the airwaves is topic of discussion between Pres. William Green and Frank Edwards, commentator on AFL air program over Mutual network for several years past.

Bottom—Pres. William Green in friendly chat with Governor A. B. Langlie of Washington State at the 1941 AFL Convention in Seattle, Washington.

William Green, LL.D., flanked by Ohio's Governor Frank Lausche, holding parchment which initiated him into honorary fraternity of Kenyon College, Ohio.

Top—Throughout the 1948 campaign when all odds were weighing down heavily against President Truman's re-election, organized labor alone stood firmly by him. Shown above is Pres. William Green gripping the hand of the young liberal senator from Minnesota, Hubert H. Humphrey, a tireless campaigner who fought along with labor, farmers and independent voters for the Fair Deal victory.

Bottom—President Green with a group of youngsters and H. J. Heintz 2nd, vice chairman of Community Chests of America, complete a "red feather" tour in the day nursery of Friendship House in Washington, D. C., September 30, 1948, to mark opening of Community Chest Campaigns throughout the country.

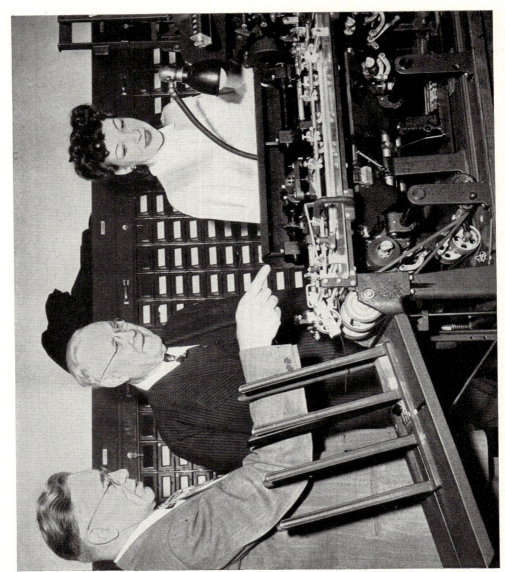

H. A. Bradley, president of International Chemical Workers Union, chaperons President William Green on a tour through a chemical plant in Akron, Ohio.

Richard F. Walsh, president of Stage and Moving Picture Machine Operators, gets "half-century" happy wishes from (l. to r.) Eric Johnston, Pres. William Green, and Ralph Wright, Assistant Secretary U. S. Department of Labor, at birthday party in March, 1950.

131

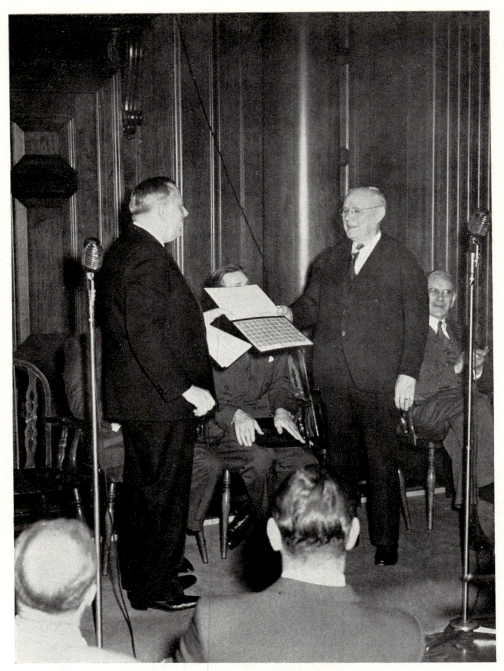

President William Green receives first batch of Samuel Gompers postage stamps from Postmaster-General Donaldson as United States pays homage to the memory of the founder of the Federation during his birthday centennial year.

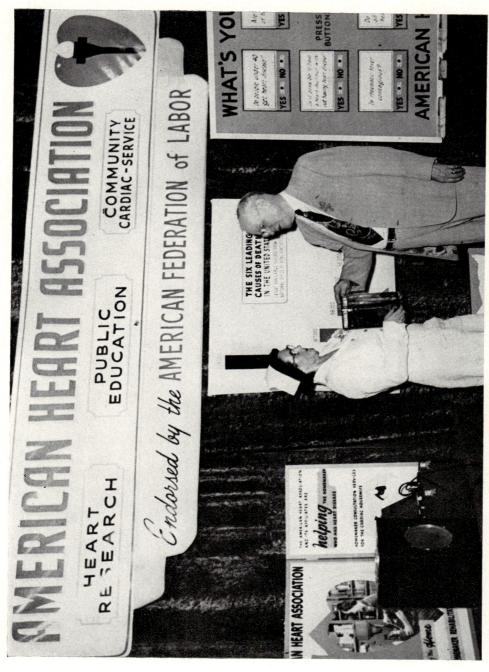

With finger on cardiometer, President William Green inspects special exhibit of the American Heart Association in March, 1950. The heart "conservation" movement is receiving nationwide AFL endorsement.

President Green is seen "shooting" a few introductory lines to "With These Hands," the Ladies' Garment Workers' historic film which was screened in 1950. The AFL chieftain appears quite relaxed and "at home" with the mike.

How Americans register their voices politically. Pres. Green shown testing "ballot secrecy" as he draws curtain over latest style voting machine, union-labor-made from A to Z, at a recent Union Industries Show.

President William Green leads applause to salient remark by President Truman at Gompers Centennial Dinner, January 5, 1951 in Washington. (L. to r.) are: U. S. Vice-President Alben W. Barkley, Mrs. Barkley, William Green, the President, George Meany, and Secretary of State Dean Acheson, who also spoke. The dinner wound up a year of Gompers memorial activities throughout the nation.

Dr. Edward J. Sparling (left), president of Roosevelt College of Chicago, meets with top labor leaders interested in progressive education, Philip Murray, CIO president, William Green, AFL president, and Albert J. Hayes, head of International Machinists' Union, to promote drive for a Samuel Gompers Memorial Fund to be presented to Roosevelt College on behalf of labor. President Hayes (right) is heading the drive.

At dedication ceremonies on October 27, 1951, of Gompers Square in Washington, D. C., in honor of the founder of the AFL, President Truman served notice that he will "renew his fight with Congress for tougher price controls." Left of President Truman is his daughter Margaret; AFL president Green is at his right.

President William Green opens the annual Union Industries Show in May, 1952, at Boston, Massachusetts. Surrounding the AFL president are members of the Executive Council who met in Boston that month, and several New England labor leaders.

AT HOME AND ABROAD

President Green adds another trophy to his vast collection as he receives from Julius Hochman, ILGWU vice-president, an ornamental eight-light candlestick, a gift from the ORT World Organization, a society dedicated to the rehabilitation and retraining for useful occupations and citizenship of displaced and disinherited youngsters. Adolph Held, chairman of American Labor Division of ORT, is at left.

Clement Attlee, British Labor Party leader and member of the War Cabinet in 1941, seen conferring with AFL President William Green while visiting the U. S. A. in November of that year to attend meeting of the International Labor Organization.

At luncheon-conference in San Francisco, initiated by Jewish Labor Committee, during formative days of the United Nations, President William Green discusses basic global issues with British Laborite George Tomlinson (right) and M. J. Coldwell, CCF leader of Canada. Subject: freedom charter for world minorities.

"We Hail and Honor"—proclaims the plaque tendered to President William Green at the 1947 convention of the AFL at San Francisco by the Jewish Labor Committee, Catholic Interracial Council and the Negro Labor Committee. Charles S. Zimmerman, ILGWU vice president, and Philip A. Randolph, president Brotherhood of Sleeping Car Porters, make the presentation.

President Green grasps hand of Isaac Ben-Zvi, ardent laborite and member of Israeli Parliament (Kneset) at AFL 1948 convention in Cincinnati, Ohio.

Bronze plaque presented to President William Green after conclusion of address at 48th national convention of Workmen's Circle, largest Jewish labor fraternal order, in Boston, Massachusetts. The late Joseph Baskin, the Circle's general secretary, made the presentation. R. Schwartz, national supervisor of Denver TB Ex-Patients Home, in center.

President Green looks contentedly at the souvenir folder entitled "The San Diego Story" sent to him as a memento of his visit on Labor Day 1949 to the Mission Bay Labor Jubilee.

Shown above (l. to r.) are: David Dubinsky, ILGWU president, AFL secretary-treasurer George Meany, President William Green, and George M. Harrison, president of Railway Mail and Steamship Clerks' Brotherhood, about to depart on board the "Ile de France" November 19, 1949, to help found the International Confederation of Free Trade Unions.

Top—President Green in midst of delegation from Histadrut, Israeli Labor Federation, which visited the United States in 1949.

Bottom—While in London, England, in December 1949, President William Green had been invited to take part in the opening ceremony of a hospital built in a working-class sector of the British metropolis.

President William Green in hearty handshake with Walter P. Reuther, United Auto Workers' president (CIO), as they met at London, at the congress of free labor unions which resulted in formation of ICFTU early in December, 1949.

At the world labor assembly where the International Confederation of Free Trade Unions was born at the London County Hall in the early days of December, 1949. The entire AFL delegation, with President William Green and secretary-treasurer George Meany (extreme lower right) watching proceedings attentively from rising level of seats.

To help settlers in new Jewish State—Discussing plans for enlisting further moral and material support for Israel and the hundreds of thousands of refugee settlers seeking to build homes there; above are (l. to r.): former Secretary of Labor Lewis B. Schwellenbach, Max Zaritsky, ex-president of the Hatters and Millinery Workers International Union, President William Green, and Nelson Rockefeller.

Top—Two Indian labor leaders, who recently spent some time in the United States, paid their respects to William Green while visiting Washington.

Bottom—At AFL-CIO luncheon, July, 1950, for Belgian labor guests. Shown (l. to r.) are: Philip Kaiser, assistant secretary U. S. Department of Labor, Josef Keuleers, Prof. Christian High School for Workers, Belgium, President Green, Nathalis De Bock, secretary-general Labor Federation of Belgium.

President William Green is flanked by Miss Inge Hauptmanns, Duesseldorf, and Miss Ruth Eva Koehn, Berlin, two of a group of German trade union youth leaders to visit AFL headquarters in October, 1950, during a 90-day study tour of United States. Others in the photo include AFL International Representative George P. Delaney; Florian Ammer, Augsburg; Karl-Heinz Boesche, Kassel; Willy Bopp, Munich; Theodor Falk, George Gebhardt, Erwin Schoenleben, Nuernberg; Erich Groha, Schweinfurt-on-Main; Adalbert Hoehne, Bremen; Eberhard Pomierski, Schongau.